STUDENT NOTES

to accompany

Gitman
PRINCIPLES OF MANAGERIAL FINANCE

STUDENT NOTES

to accompany

Gitman
PRINCIPLES OF MANAGERIAL FINANCE
Seventh Edition

Thomas J. Liesz
Western State College

HarperCollinsCollegePublishers

Student Notes to accompany Gitman, PRINCIPLES OF MANAGERIAL FINANCE, Seventh Edition

Copyright © 1994 HarperCollins College Publishers

ISBN: 0-06-502329-3

94 95 96 97 98   9 8 7 6 5 4 3 2 1

Three Important Liquidity Measures

4-9

Net Working Capital (NWC)

NWC = Current Assets - Current Liabilities

Current Ratio (CR)

$$CR = \frac{Current\ Assets}{Current\ Liabilities}$$

Quick (Acid-Test) Ratio (QR)

$$QR = \frac{Current\ Assets - Inventory}{Current\ Liabilities}$$

4-10

Analyzing Activity

- **Activity is a more sophisticated analysis of a firm's liquidity, evaluating the speed with which certain accounts are converted into sales or cash; also measures a firm's efficiency**

Five Important Activity Measures

4-11

Inventory Turnover (IT)

$$IT = \frac{Cost\ of\ Goods\ Sold}{Inventory}$$

Average Collection Period (ACP)

$$ACP = \frac{Accounts\ Receivable}{Annual\ Sales/360}$$

Average Payment Period (APP)

$$APP = \frac{Accounts\ Payable}{Annual\ Purchases/360}$$

Fixed Asset Turnover (FAT)

$$FAT = \frac{Sales}{Net\ Fixed\ Assets}$$

Total Asset Turnover (TAT)

$$TAT = \frac{Sales}{Total\ Assets}$$

4-12

Analyzing Debt

- Debt is a true "double-edged" sword as it allows for the generation of profits with the use of other people's (creditors) money, but creates claims on earnings with a higher priority than those of the firm's owners

- Financial Leverage is a term for the magnification of risk and return resulting from the use of fixed-cost financing such as debt and preferred stock

TABLE OF CONTENTS

Introduction

Introduction

Student Notes to accompany Gitman's *Principles of Managerial Finance, Seventh Edition* was created to assist you with note taking during lectures and classroom discussions. Thanks to the comments and suggestions we received regarding our first effort, we feel that this current edition does a better job of accomplishing this purpose. Each chapter is a detailed outline chapter material and paralells your instructors lecture outlines and transparencies.

Student Notes consists mainly of summaries of the textbook material, but includes additional examples and discussion material for each chapter. Each chapter concludes with a set of Discussion Problems. The **Student Notes** will provide an outline of the lectures as well as providing diagrams, and timelines that will allow you to concentrate on the concepts being discussed in class, rather than furiously copying down data, formulas, and graphs.

The **Student Notes** are probably more comprehensive than what your instructor can comfortably cover in the time allocated to each chapter. We feel however, that it was better to provide more material and allow instructors to choose from the material available.

We want to thank all of our colleagues who provided us with constructive criticism and helpful suggestions, especially Mark Chockalingan and Maurice P. Corrigan. Please continue to assist us in our endeavor to make **Student Notes** as useful to you as possible.

Lastly, we extend or appreciation to Lorna Dotts for her usual superb job in preparing the manuscript for this supplement.

Thomas Liesz   Lawrence J. Gitman
Western State College   *San Diego State University*
Gunnison, CO   LaJolla, California

1-1

The Role of Finance and the Financial Manager

- **Introduction**
- **Finance As An Area Of Study**
- **Basic Forms Of Business Organization**
- **The Managerial Finance Function**
- **Key Activities Of The Financial Manager**
- **Goal Of The Financial Manager**
- **The Role Of Ethics**

Finance as an Area of Study

1-2

- **What is Finance?**
  - **The art and science of managing money**
  - **The process, institutions, markets, and instruments involved in the transfer of money between individuals, businesses, and governments form the foundation of the study of finance**

Major Areas in Finance

1-3

- *Financial services*
  - Banking and related institutions
    - » Loan Officers; Retail Bank Manager; Trust Officers; Money Managers
  - Personal financial planning
    - » Financial planners
  - Investments
    - » Brokers; Analysts; Portfolio Managers; Investment Bankers
  - Real Estate and Insurance
    - » Agent Bankers; Property Manager; Mortgage Banker; Broker; Insurance Specialist; Appraisers; Underwriters
- *Managerial finance*
  - Budgeting   Investment Analysis
  - Financial Forecasting   Cash Management
  - Credit Administration   Funds Procurement
  - Exchange Rate Risk Hedging

The Study of Managerial Finance

1-4

An understanding of the theories, concepts, techniques, and practices inherent to the financial manager's activities will give you insight to the role finance plays in managerial decision making

The Study of Managerial Finance

1-5

The managerial finance principles presented, while focused upon profit-seeking organizations, are equally applicable to public and other non-profit organizations

These principles are also applicable to personal financial decisions

Basic Forms of Business Organization

1-6

•Sole Proprietorships
•Partnerships
•Corporations

Copyright ©1994, HarperCollins Publishers

Basic Forms of Business Organization

1-7

■Sole Proprietorships

- –Business owned and controlled by one person
- –Most common form of ownership structure
- –Sole proprietor has unlimited liability

Basic Forms of Business Organization

1-8

• Partnerships

- –*General partnership* is a business owned and controlled by two or more persons, each with equal responsibility for debts and unlimited liability
- –*Limited partnership* is a business owned and controlled by two or more persons in which one or more partners is designated as having liability limited to their individual investment in the business

Basic Forms of Business Organization

1-9

■Corporations

- ■An association of stockholders created under state law and regarded as a legal entity
- ■Stockholders are the true owners; they have limited liability
- ■Board of Directors is elected by the stockholders
- ■President or CEO is hired by the Board of Directors

Corporate Organization

1-10

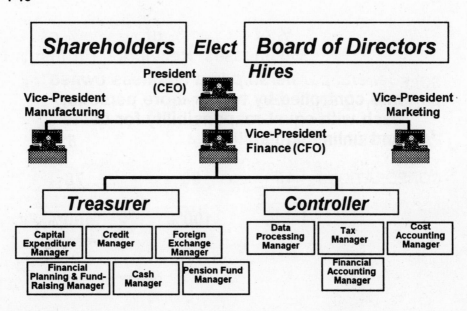

Strengths and Weaknesses of the Basic Legal forms of Business Organization

1-11

	Strengths	Weaknesses
Sole Proprietorship	Owner gets all profits Low organizational costs Income taxed as personal income Secrecy Ease of dissolution	Owner has *unlimited liability* Limited fund raising powers Difficulty to give employees long-run career opportunities Lack of continuity when proprietor dies
Partnership	Can raise more funds than proprietorships More managerial skill Can retain good employees Income taxed as personal income of partners	Owners have *unlimited liability* When a partner dies, partnership is dissolved Difficult to liquidate or transfer partnership Difficult to achieve large scale operations
Corporation	Owners have *limited liability* Can achieve large size Ownership easily transferable Long life of firm Can hire professional managers Certain tax advantages	Taxes generally higher More expensive to organize than other business forms Subject to greater government regulation

Business Organization Statistics

1-12

	% of Businesses	% of Receipts	% of Profits
SOLE PROPRIETORSHIPS	75%	8%	17%
PARTNERSHIPS	10	4	5
CORPORATIONS	15	88	78
	100%	100%	100%

The Managerial Finance Function

1-13

• An Organizational View

- –An understanding of finance is important for individuals involved in all areas of an organization since most business decisions are measured in financial terms

- –The allocation of resources within an organization is usually based in large part upon the financial merits of each proposal

The Managerial Finance Function

1-14

Relationship to Economics

From *macroeconomics* the financial manager must understand the economic framework within which the firm operates

From *microeconomics* the financial manager must utilize economic theories in decision making, particularly marginal analysis

The Managerial Finance Function
1-15

Relationship to Accounting

The emphasis of the financial manager is on *cash flows*

Decision making

While accountants certainly make decisions, their primary activity is gathering and presenting financial data

The financial manager's primary activity is decision making, after utilizing accounting and other data

Example
1-16

The Sandberg Corporation had the following financial results last year:

- **Sales:** $100,000 (50% still uncollected)
- **Cost of Goods:** $ 60,000 (all paid in full under supplier terms)
- **Expenses:** $ 30,000 (all paid in full)

Income Statement Summary

1-17

	ACCRUAL METHOD	CASH METHOD
Sales	$100,000	$ 50,000
-COGS	- 60,000	-60,000
Gross Margin	40,000	(10,000)
-Expenses	-30,000	-30,000
Net Profit/(Loss)	$ 10,000	$(40,000)

From the accounting standpoint Sandberg Corporation appears to be in good shape; from the managerial finance standpoint, it is in trouble - it had greater cash outflows than inflows

Key Activities of the Financial Manager

1-18

Performing Financial Analysis and Planning

- **Monitoring the firm's financial condition through financial data transformation**
- **Evaluating the need for changes in productive capacity**
- **Evaluating the need for changes in financing**

Key Activities of the Financial Manager

1-19

Making Investing and Financing Decisions can best be shown by the balance sheet

BALANCE SHEET

ASSETS	LIABILITIES AND EQUITY
(Investing Decisions)	(Financing Decisions)
Investments	financing sources include:
in resources	borrowing and owner-provided
Establish and maintain	Establish and maintain
proper mix of current	proper mix of current and
and fixed assets	long-term liabilities and equity

The Financial Manager and TQM

1-20

- **TQM (*Total Quality Management*) is the application of quality principles to all aspects of a firm's operations with an emphasis on achieving greater levels of efficiency and needs satisfaction for both internal and external customers**

- **The financial manager contributes to TQM by ensuring that budgets are available on a timely basis, financial analyses are performed at an appropriate level, and decisions are made quickly**

Goal of the Financial Manager

1-21

• Maximize Profit?

- This technique ignores:
  - Timing
  - Cash flows
  - Risk
    - »Risk and return
    - »Stockholders are generally *risk-averse* and expect higher returns for assuming higher levels of risk

Goal of the Financial Manager

1-22

• Maximizing Shareholder Wealth

- The goal of the firm is to maximize the wealth of the stockholders by maximizing the price of the firm's stock
- The price of stock is a function of the timing of cash flows, the magnitude of the cash flows, and the risk associated with realizing the cash flows

Goal of the Financial Manager

1-23

■**Preserving Stakeholder Wealth**

■Stakeholders include all groups of individuals who have a direct economic link to the firm, including: Employees; Customers; Suppliers; Creditors

■The "Stakeholder View" prescribes that the firm makes a conscious effort to avoid actions that could be detrimental to the wealth positions of its stakeholders

■Such a view is considered to be "socially responsible"

Goal of the Financial Manager

1-24

• **The Agency Issue**

–Since managers are (most often) nonowners of a firm, the potential of their placing personal goals ahead of corporate goals creates an *agency problem*

–Market forces tend to ensure the competence of management and minimize agency problems

–To minimize the agency problem, stockholders incur *agency costs*

Goal of the Financial Manager

1-25

• The Role of Ethics

–Ethics - the standards of conduct or moral judgment - have become an overriding issue in both our society and the financial community

Goal of the Financial Manager

1-26

■The Role of Ethics

■To assess the ethical viability of a proposed action, ask:

■Does the action unfairly single out an individual or group?

■Does the action violate the moral or legal rights of any individual or group?

■Does the action conform to accepted moral standards?

■Are there alternative courses of action that are less likely to cause actual or potential harm?

DISCUSSION PROBLEM

1-27

- **Hal Nelson, a student of finance, wishes to rank the three basic forms of business organization on a number of factors. He has created the chart shown below. Help him complete it, using a 1 for best, a 2 for the middle, and a 3 for the worst case. Use the same number to indicate a tie.**

1-28

DISCUSSION PROBLEM

FACTOR	SOLE PROPRIETORSHIP	GENERAL PARTNERSHIP	CORPORATION
1. Access To Funds			
2. Ease and Cost of Organization			
3. Managerial Control			
4. Business Continuity			
5. Liability For Business Debts			
6. Taxation			
7. Transferability Of Ownership			

The Operating Environment of the Firm

2-1

- **Financial Institutions And Markets: An Overview**
- **The Capital Market**
- **Interest Rates And Required Returns**
- **Business Taxation**

Financial Institutions and Markets: An Overview

2-2

Introduction

Business firms operate within the framework of a financial system that is made up of suppliers of funds and demanders of funds

Linking the suppliers and demanders of funds are intermediaries, called financial institutions, and financial markets

Financial Institutions and Markets: An Overview
2-3

Financial Institutions

Financial Institutions channel the savings of individuals, business, and government into loans and investments

Key Participants in Financial Transactions

Major Financial Institutions

Changing Role of Financial Institutions

Financial Institutions and Markets: An Overview
2-4

Financial Markets

The relationship between institutions and markets is a direct and strong one as financial institutions are active participants in both the money and the capital market as both suppliers and demanders of funds

The Money Market

The money market is not a physical entity

The operation of the Money Market

Participants in the Money Market

The Eurocurrency Market

Copyright ©1994, HarperCollins Publishers

Flow of Funds

2-5

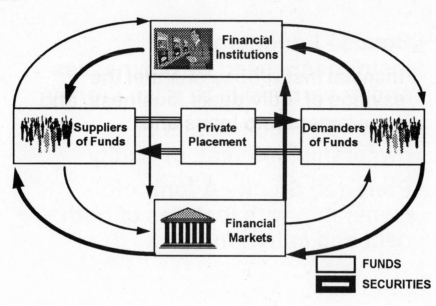

The Capital Market

2-6

- **The capital market is a financial relationship created by a number of institutions and arrangements that allows the suppliers and demanders of long-term funds to make transactions**

Key Securities

2-7

- **Bonds - Long-term debt instruments used by businesses and governments to raise money**
- **Common Stock - Units of ownership, interest, or equity**
- **Preferred Stock - A form of ownership with features of both debt and common stock**

Major Securities Exchanges

2-8

- **Organized Securities Exchanges are organizations that act as markets for previously issued securities**
  - **They are secondary markets**
  - **The dominant exchanges are the *New York Stock Exchange* and the *American Stock Exchange***
  - **Trading is accomplished through an auction process**
  - **Once placed, an order to buy or sell is usually executed in a matter of minutes**

Major Securities Exchanges

2-9

■The Over-the-Counter (OTC) Exchange is a market for the purchase and sale of outstanding securities not listed on an organized exchanges

　■It is a *secondary market*

　■OTC dealers are linked through the NASDAQ System

　■The prices at which securities are traded result from competitive bids and negotiations

　■The OTC is also a *primary market*

Major Securities Exchanges

2-10

■International Capital Markets

　■The *Eurobond Market* is the functional equivalent of a long-term *Eurocurrency market*

　■The Foreign Bond Market is one in which a foreign corporation or government issues bonds

　■An International Equity Market has emerged that allows corporations to sell large blocks of shares simultaneously to investors in several different countries

The Role of Securities Exchanges

2-11

- **Create a continuous, liquid market in which demanders of funds can obtain needed financing**
- **Create an *efficient market* that allocates funds to their most productive uses**

The Role of the Investment Banker

2-12

- Investment bankers serve as intermediaries between the issuers and purchasers of new security issues
  - The *investment banker* purchases securities from issuers and resells them in the primary market
  - Investment bankers are generally used regardless of whether the sale of securities is a *public offering* or a *private placement*

Interest Rates and Required Rates of Return

2-13

Interest Rate Fundamentals

- The interest rate is the "price" of borrowed funds
- The required return is the owner's expected return
- The *real rate of interest* (k^*) is the cost of money that balances the supply of and demand for funds
- The *risk-free rate of interest* (R_F) represents the real rate of interest plus inflationary expectations
- The *nominal rate of interest* (k) is the actual rate of interest charged by the supplier of funds

2-14

Equation

$$k^* + IP + RP$$

or

the risk free rate + a risk premium (RP)

Interest Rates and Required Returns

2-15

- **Term Structure of Interest Rates**
  - More commonly known as a *yield curve*, it shows the relationship between the interest rate, or rate of return, and the time to maturity of securities with similar issuer characteristics
  - Yield curves can be downward-sloping, flat, or upward sloping
  - The three theories of term structure are the expectations hypothesis, liquidity preference theory, and market segmantation theory
  - A *normal yield curve* is upward-sloping

Interest Rates and Required Returns

2-16

• Risk and Return

- A positive relationship exists between risk and nominal or expected return
- The actual return earned on a security will affect the subsequent actions of investors
- Investors must be compensated for accepting greater risk with the expectation of greater return

Business Taxation

2-17

Ordinary Income Versus Capital Gain

- Two types of income can be earned by business firms

  - Ordinary income; Capital gains

- Each type of income is treated the same under current tax law

- One goal of the financial manager is to minimize tax liability and thereby increase cash inflows

S Corporations

2-18

- Subchapter S of the Internal Revenue Code permits corporations meeting specific requirements, and having 35 or less stockholders, to be taxed like partnerships

- The S Corporation enjoys most of the other benefits of a corporation, particularly limited liability

- About 20 percent of small business corporations have chosen the S option

DISCUSSION PROBLEMS

2-19

- **A 3-year treasury note carries a current yield to maturity of 9%. If the real rate of interest is 4% and inflation is expected to be 3% over the next two years, what is the expected rate of inflation in year 3?**

SOLUTION

2-20

DISCUSSION PROBLEMS

2-21

Ben Johnson, a student of finance, travels to the
local bank with the president of his university.
Each applies for a loan. Ben borrows $40,000
over five years to buy a new Corvette. The
university president borrows $5,000 over one
year to purchase a set of diamond-studded
earrings. As they drive back to campus, they
are delighted that each had his loan approved.
Ben says, "I think that 23.5% rate I got for the
'Vette was pretty good." The president replies,
"Jumpin' Jehosaphat, my rate was 8.75%; why
the big difference?" In terms of the risk
premium, what should Ben's response be?

DISCUSSION PROBLEMS

2-22

Ben's girlfriend, Suzy Smith, was assigned by her finance instructor to draw the current yield curve. Suzy looked through the local newspaper and found that the local credit union was charging 10% for 60-month car loans, a nearby bank was paying 7% for one-year CD's, the neighborhood savings and loan had 30-year fixed-rate mortgages for 12%, and the university was offering 90-day loans to students for 8%. If Suzy used this data to draw the yield curve would it be valid? Why or why not?

3-1 *Financial Statements, Depreciation, and Cash Flow*

• The Stockholders' Report

• Basic Financial Statements

• Depreciation

• Analyzing The Firm's Cash Flow

3-2 *Financial Statements, Depreciation, and Cash Flow*

• THE STOCKHOLDERS' REPORT: Basic Definitions

- Stockholders' Report
- Generally Accepted Accounting Principles (GAAP)
- Financial Accounting Standards Board (FASB)
- Publicly held corporations
- Securities and Exchange Commission

Contents of a Stockholders' Report

3-3

- **Letter to Stockholders**
- **Financial Statements**
  - –Income Statement
  - –Balance Sheet
  - –Statement of Retained Earnings
  - –Statement of Cash Flows
- **Notes to Financial Statements**
- **Other Featured Information**

Basic Financial Statements

3-4

- **Income Statement**
  - –The Income Statement evaluates the operating performance of a firm over some period of time by matching its accomplishments (revenue or sales) with its efforts (cost of goods sold and other expenses)
  - –Most income statements cover a one-year period

Baker Corporation Income Statement ($000) For the Year Ended Dec. 31, 1994

3-5

Sales revenue		$1,700
Less: COGS		1,000
Gross profits		$ 700
Less: Operating Expenses		
Selling expense	$ 80	
General expenses	150	
Depreciation expenses	100	
Total operating expense		330
Operating profits		$ 370
Less: Interest expense		70
Net profit before taxes		$ 300
Less Taxes (40%)		120
Net profit after taxes		$ 180
Less: preferred stock dividends		10
Earnings available for common stockholders		$ 170
Earnings per share		$ 1.70

Basic Financial Statements

3-6

• Balance Sheet

– The Balance Sheet is a statement of financial position at a given point in time

– It is important to understand the distinction between short-term and long-term balance sheet accounts

Baker Corporation Balance Sheets

3-7

Assets	1994	1993
Current assets	$ 400	$ 300
Cash	600	200
Marketable securities	400	500
Accounts receivable	600	900
Inventories	$ 2,000	$ 1,900
Total current assets		
Gross fixed assets (at cost)	$ 1,200	$ 1,050
Land and buildings	850	800
Machinery and equipment	300	220
Furniture and fixtures	100	80
Vehicles	50	50
Other (Including leases)		
Total gross fixed assets	$2,500	$2,200
Less: accumulated depreciation	1,300	1,200
Net fixed assets	$1,200	$1,000
Total assets	$ 3,200	$ 2,900

3-8

Liabilities and Equity	1994	1993
Current liabilities		
Accounts payable	$ 700	$ 500
Notes payable	600	700
Accruals	100	200
Total current liabilities	$ 1,400	$ 1,400
Long-term debt	$ 600	$ 400
Total liabilities	$ 2,000	$ 1,800
Stockholder's equity		
Preferred stock	$ 100	$ 100
Common stock- $1.20 par, 100,000 shares outstanding in '93 & '94	120	120
Paid-in capital in excess of par on common stock	380	380
Retained earnings	600	500
Total stockholders equity	$ 1,200	$ 1,100
Total liabilities & stockholder's equity	$ 3,200	$ 2,900

Basic Financial Statements

3-9

- ## Statement of Retained Earnings

  - Statement of Retained Earnings analyzes changes in the retained earnings account for a given period of time; it is the link between the income statement and the balance sheet

Basic Financial Statements

3-10

- ## Statement of Cash Flows

  - The Statement of Cash Flows summarizes the flow of cash receipts and cash payments of a firm during a given period of time

    » Provides more understandable information

    » Organizes cash transactions into the three primary activities of finance: operating, investment, and financing cash flows

Depreciation

3-11

The allocation of the historical (acquisition) cost of property, plant, and equipment to the particular periods of time that benefit from the use of these fixed assets

» 1. Straight-line

» 2. Double-declining balance

» 3. Sum-of-the-year's-digits

Depreciation and Cash Flows

3-12

- **Depreciation is an example of a noncash charge**

  Net Profit After Taxes
  + <u>Noncash Charges</u>
  = Cash Flow From Operations

- **Depreciation allows the firm to reduce its tax liability and thus keep more of its cash inflows**

Rounded Depreciation Percentages by Recovery Year Using MACRS for First Four Property Classes

3-13

	Percentage by Recovery Year			
Recovery Year	3-year	5-year	7-year	10-year
1	33%	20%	14%	10%
2	45%	32%	25%	18%
3	15%	19%	18%	14%
4	7%	12%	12%	12%
5		12%	9%	9%
6		5%	9%	8%
7			9%	7%
8			4%	6%
9				6%
10				6%
11				4%
Totals	100%	100%	100%	100%

3-14

Copyright ©1994, HarperCollins Publishers

Cash Flows

(1) Operating Flows   **(2) Investment Flows**

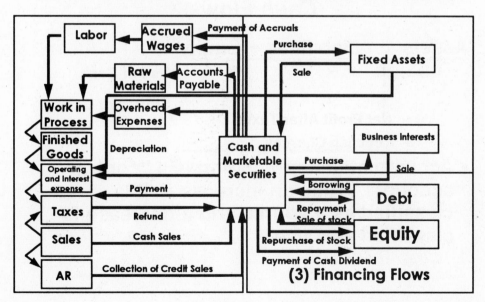

The Sources and Uses of Cash

3-15

SOURCES   USES

Decrease in any asset   **Increase in any asset**
Increase in any liability **Decrease in any liability**
Net profits after taxes   **Net loss**
Depreciation and other   **Dividends paid**
   noncash charges   **Repurchase or**
Sale of stock   **retirement of stock**

Developing the Statement of Cash Flows

3-16

Assets	Liabilities + Equity	
+	-	= Use of Cash
-	+	= Source of Cash

• **Accumulated depreciation is a "contra account". Thus an increase in it is classified as a source and a decrease is classified as a use**

DISCUSSION PROBLEM

3-17

Rich Ables, a student of finance, is trying to prepare a Sources and
Uses of Cash Statement for the Torbert Company. He has
calculated the changes for the period listed below. Help him
classify the changes. How can you check your answer?

ITEM	CHANGE	SOURCE(S) OR USE(U)?
Cash	- 300	_____
Accounts Receivable	+2,100	_____
Inventory	- 900	_____
Gross Fixed Assets	+2,700	_____
Depreciation	+3,000	_____
Accounts Payable	+ 900	_____
Accruals	- 300	_____
Long-Term Debt	- 600	_____
Net Profit	+1,800	_____
Dividends	+1,200	_____

3-18   # DISCUSSION PROBLEM

The items listed below were found on a recent statement of cash
flows of the American Telephone and Telegraph Company (AT&T).
For each item, indicate which section of the statement should
contain the item - the operating(O), investment (I), or financing(F)
section-and whether it is a source(S) or use(U).

	Section	S/U
a. Increase in long-term debt	_____	_____
b. Net income	_____	_____
c. Dividends paid	_____	_____
d. Retirement of long-term debt	_____	_____
e. Increase in short term borrowing	_____	_____

The Analysis of Financial Statements

4-1

- **The Use Of Financial Ratios**
- **Analyzing Liquidity**
- **Analyzing Activity**
- **Analyzing Debt**
- **Analyzing Profitability**
- **A Complete Ratio Analysis**

The Analysis of Financial Statements

4-2

- **THE USE OF FINANCIAL RATIOS**
  - Financial Ratio is a relative measure that facilitates the evaluation of efficiency or condition of a particular aspect of a firm's operations and status
  - Ratio Analysis involves methods of calculating and interpreting financial ratios in order to assess a firm's performance and status

4-3

Example

• Year End	(1) Current Assets	(2) Current Liabilities	(3) (1)/(2) Current Ratio
1993	$550,000	$500,000	1.10
1994	$550,000	$600,000	.92

4-4 *Interested Parties*

Three sets of parties are interested in ratio analysis:

•Shareholders

•Creditors

•Management

4-5   *Types of Ratio Comparisons*

There are two types of ratio comparisons that can be made:

- **Cross-Sectional Analysis**

- **Time-Series Analysis**
  - –Combined Analysis uses both types of analysis to assess a firm's trends versus its competitors or the industry

4-6   *Words of Caution Regarding Ratio Analysis*

- **A single ratio rarely tells enough to make a sound judgment**

- **Financial statements used in ratio analysis must be from similar points in time**

- **Audited financial statements are more reliable than unaudited statements**

- **The financial data used to compute ratios must be developed in the same manner**

- **Inflation can distort comparisons**

4-7   *Groups of Financial Ratios*

☞**Liquidity**

☞**Activity**

☞**Debt**

☞**Profitability**

4-8   *Analyzing Liquidity*

• **Liquidity refers to the solvency of the firm's overall financial position, i.e. a "liquid firm" is one that can easily meet its short-term obligations as they come due**

4-13   *Measures of Debt*

• There are Two General Types of Debt Measures

–Degree of Indebtedness

–Ability to Service Debts

4-14   *Four Important Debt Measures*

**Debt Ratio
(DR)**

$$DR = \frac{\text{Total Liabilities}}{\text{Total Assets}}$$

**Debt-Equity Ratio
(DER)**

$$DER = \frac{\text{Long-Term Debt}}{\text{Stockholders' Equity}}$$

**Times Interest Earned
Ratio (TIE)**

$$TIE = \frac{\text{Earnings Before Interest \& Taxes (EBIT)}}{\text{Interest}}$$

**Fixed Payment Coverage
Ratio (FPC)**

$$FPC = \frac{\text{Earnings Before Interest \& Taxes + Lease Payments}}{\text{Interest + Lease Payments} + \{(\text{Principal Payments + Preferred Stock Dividends}) \times [1/(1-T)]\}}$$

4-15

Analyzing Profitability

–Profitability Measures assess the firm's ability to operate efficiently and are of concern to owners, creditors, and management

–A Common-Size Income Statement, which expresses each income statement item as a percentage of sales, allows for easy evaluation of the firm's profitability relative to sales.

4-16

Seven Basic Profitability Measures

Gross Profit Margin (GPM) $GPM = \dfrac{Gross\ Profits}{Sales}$

Operating Profit Margin (OPM) $OPM = \dfrac{Operating\ Profits\ (EBIT)}{Sales}$

Net Profit Margin (NPM) $NPM = \dfrac{Net\ Profit\ After\ Taxes}{Sales}$

Return on Total Assets (ROA) $ROA = \dfrac{Net\ Profit\ After\ Taxes}{Total\ Assets}$

Return On Equity (ROE) $ROE = \dfrac{Net\ Profit\ After\ Taxes}{Stockholders'\ Equity}$

Earnings Per Share (EPS) $EPS = \dfrac{Earnings\ Available\ for\ Common\ Stockholder's}{Number\ of\ Shares\ of\ Common\ StockOutstanding}$

Price/Earnings (P/E) Ratio $P/E = \dfrac{Market\ Price\ Per\ Share\ of\ Common\ Stock}{Earnings\ Per\ Share}$

4-17   *A Complete Ratio Analysis*

• DuPont System of Analysis

–DuPont System of Analysis is an integrative approach used to dissect a firm's financial statements and assess its financial condition

–It ties together the income statement and balance sheet to determine two summary measures of profitability, namely ROA and ROE

4-18   *DuPont System of Analysis*

• The firm's return is broken into three components:

–A profitability measure
(net profit margin)

–An efficiency measure
(total asset turnover)

–A leverage measure
(financial leverage multiplier)

4-19 *Summarizing All Ratios*

- **An approach that views all aspects of the firm's activities to isolate key areas**
- **Comparisons are made to industry standards**
    - *(cross-sectional analysis)*
- **Comparisons to the firm itself over time are also made**
    - *(time-series analysis)*

4-20 *DISCUSSION PROBLEMS*

Figures from the Zachary Corporation's common-size income statement include:

Gross Profit Margin	28.7%
Operating Profit Margin	17.5%
Taxes	5.4%
Net Profit Margin	9.6%

Find: Cost of goods sold (as a %)

   Total Operating Expense (as a %)

   Interest Expense (as a %)

DISCUSSION PROBLEMS

4-21

Set up statement with known values

Sales	100.0%
Cost of Goods Sold	_____
Gross Profit Margin	28.7%
Operating Expense	_____
Operating Profit Margin	17.5%
Interest Expense	_____
Net Profit Before Taxes	
Taxes	5.4%
Net Profit Margin	9.6%

DISCUSSION PROBLEMS

4-22

Compute missing values

- Cost of Goods Sold   =   =
- Total Operating Expense   =   =
- Net Profit Before Taxes   =   =
- Interest Expense   =   =

DISCUSSION PROBLEMS

4-23

- Using the following information on the J.T. Nissa Company, compute the firm's return on equity, using the modified DuPont formula

BALANCE SHEET (000's)

Current Assets	$1,000	Current Liabilities	$ 600
Fixed Assets	5,000	Long-term Liabilities	1,500
Total Assets	$6,000	Common stock (at par)	2,000
		Paid-in Capital	1,000
		Retained Earnings	900
		Total Liabilities	$6,000

DISCUSSION PROBLEMS

4-24

INCOME STATEMENT (000's)

Net Sales	$12,000
COGS	-7,100
Gross Profit	4,900
Operating Expense	-3,000
Operating Profit	1,900
Interest	-200
Net Profit Before Taxes	1,700
Taxes (40%)	-680
Net Profit	$ 1,020

DISCUSSION PROBLEMS

4-25

$$ROE = \text{Net Profit Margin} \times \text{Total Assets Turnover} \times \text{Financial Leverage}$$

$$= \frac{\text{Net Profit}}{\text{Sales}} \times \frac{\text{Sales}}{\text{Total Assets}} \times \frac{\text{Total Assets}}{\text{Stockholder's Equity}}$$

$$= \frac{}{} \times \frac{}{} \times \frac{}{} =$$

$$ROE =$$

OR
$$ROE = \frac{\text{Net Profit}}{\text{Stockholder's Equity}} = \frac{}{} =$$

The Time Value of Money

5-1

- The role of time value in finance
- Future value of a single amount
- Future value of an annuity
- Present value of a single amount
- Present value of cash flow streams
- Special applications of time value

5-2   *The Time Value of Money*

Most financial decisions involve benefits and costs that are spread out over time - the time value of money establishes a relationship between cash flows received and/or paid at different points in time.

5-3
The Role of Time Value in Finance

- Future versus Present Value
  - *Time lines* can be used to depict cash flows
  - *Compounding* is used to find future value
  - *Discounting* is used to find present value
- Computational aids
  - Financial tables of interest factors
  - Business/Financial calculators

The Concept of Future Values

5-4

Terminology:

Future Value

Compounded Interest

Principal

Simple Interest

5-5

Justin Jones has borrowed $1000 from his grandmother for two years at 8% simple interest. How much will Justin pay Granny in two years?

Simple Interest

5-6

Justin Jones has borrowed $1000 from his grandmother for two years at 8% simple interest. How much will Justin pay Granny in two years?

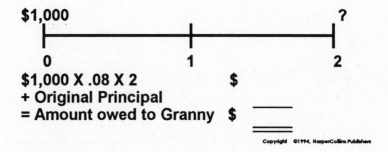

$1,000   ?

|——————————|——————————|

0   1   2

$1,000 X .08 X 2 $

+ Original Principal

= Amount owed to Granny $ _____

5-7   *Compounded Interest*

Granny just found Justin's finance book and discovered the concept of compounded interest. At 8% annual compounded interest, how much will Justin owe Granny at the end of two years?

Solution

5-8

5-9   *Future Value Formula*

$$FV_n = PV\ (1+k)^n$$

FV_n = Future value at the end of the year n
PV = Present value, or original principal amount
k = Annual rate of interest paid
n = Number of periods (usually years) separating
          the present value and the future value, or
          number of years the money is left on deposit

Compounded Interest Example

5-10

**If Rita Brown deposits $800 today in an account
paying 9% annual interest, how much will
she have at the end of three years?**

Compounded Interest Example

5-11

If Rita Brown deposits $800 today in an account paying 9% annual interest, how much will she have at the end of three years?

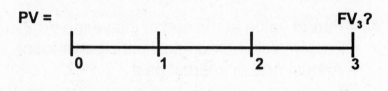

$PV =$ $FV_3?$

| | | | |
|0|1|2|3|

$PV =$ $, k =$ $, n =$

_____

A Graphic View of Future Value

5-12

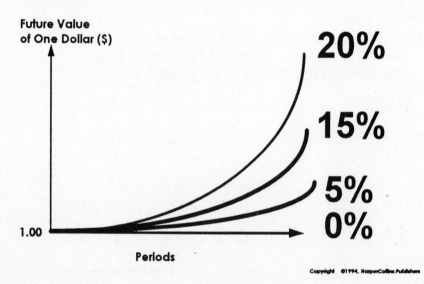

You Try One!

5-13

What is the future value of $1,000 compounded at 7% annually for nine years?

PV = $1,000   FV$_9$?

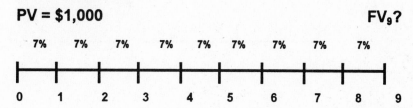

Important notes regarding FVIF tables (Table A-1)

5-14

- The FVIF$_{k,n}$ factors assume beginning-of-period cash flows

- FVIF$_{k,n}$ is always >1 (as long as k > o)

- As k ↑ , the FVIF$_{k,n}$ also ↑

- As n ↑ , the FVIF$_{k,n}$ also ↑

Example

5-15

How long will it take Dan Smits to double his $100 if he deposits it in an account earning 10% compounded annually?

Example

5-16

How long will it take Dan Smits to double his $100 if he deposits it in an account earning 10% compounded annually?

PV =   FV$_n$ =   k =

5-17   *Example*

Pete Brown received $1,000 on his tenth birthday. He plans on buying a new motorcycle on his sixteenth birthday, but figures he'll need at least $1,500 for the purchase. What is the minimum annual compound rate of interest Pete's deposit will need to earn?

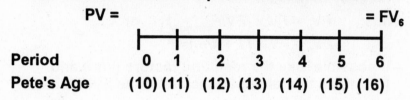

PV =   = FV$_6$

Period	0	1	2	3	4	5	6
Pete's Age	(10)	(11)	(12)	(13)	(14)	(15)	(16)

5-18   *What we know:*

PV =   ;   FV$_6$ =   ;   n =
Plug into the formula

Compounding More Frequently Than Annually
5-19

- New variable: m = number of compounding   periods per year

  - Divide k by m
  - Multiply m times n

  Thus: $FV_n = PV \times (FVIF_{k/m, m \times n})$ or

  $\quad\quad\quad FV_n = PV \times (1 + k/m)^{m \times n}$

  - If possible, use the resulting factors (k/m) and (m x n) as the table parameters in the FVIF table
  - If a resulting factor is not found on the FVIF table (such as a k of 2.5%), you must use a business/financial calculator.

5-20 *Example*

What is the future value of $1,000 deposited in an account paying 12% interest compounded quarterly after four years?

PV =   ;   k =   ,   m =   ,   n =

5-21 **Nominal And Effective Interest Rates**

- **Nominal, or stated, rates**
- **Effective, or stated, rates**
- **annual percentage rate (or APR)**
- **The effective rate (k_{eff})**

(5-22) **Equation for Effective Rate of Interest, k_{eff}**

$$k_{eff} = (1 + k/m)^m - 1$$

5-23

Example

- **Nominal Rate, k, = 12%**

Compounding Period	m	$k_{eff} = (1+k/m)^m - 1$		Effective Rate	
Annual	1	$(1 +.12/1) -1$	$= 1 +.12 -1$	$= .12$	$= 12.00\%$
Semiannual	2	$(1 + .12/2)^2 -1$	$= 1.1236 -1$	$= .1236$	$= 12.36\%$
Quarterly	4	$(1 + .12/4)^4 -1$	$= 1.1255 -1$	$= .1255$	$= 12.55\%$
Monthly	12	$(1 + .12/12)^{12} -1$	$= 1.1268 -1$	$= .1268$	$= 12.68\%$
Daily	360	$(1 + .12/360)^{360} -1$	$= 1.1275 -1$	$= .1275$	$= 12.75\%$
Continuously	∞	$(1 + .12/\infty)^\infty -1 = e^k -1$		$= .1275$	$= 12.75\%$

5-24 *Future value of an Annuity*

Types of Annuities:

Annuities

Ordinary Annuities

Annuities Due

Example

5-25

What is the future value of an ordinary, 3-year annuity of $1,000 at 10% annual compounding?

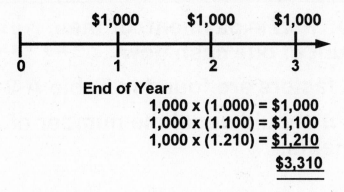

End of Year

1,000 x (1.000) = $1,000
1,000 x (1.100) = $1,100
1,000 x (1.210) = $1,210

$3,310

5-26 # *Example*

This can be rewritten as:

$1,000 x (1.000 + 1.100 + 1.210) or $1,000 x (3.310)

Find 3 periods and 10% ... 3.310 ...

Basic future value of an annuity formula
5-27

$$FVA_n = PMT \times (FVIFA_{k,n})$$

Where: *PMT* = payment, or the amount of one cash flow

FVIFA factors are found in Table A-2

Note: *n* should equal the number of payments!

5-28

Example

What is the future value of an ordinary, eight-year annuity of $100 compounded at 7% annually?

$FVA_8 = ?$

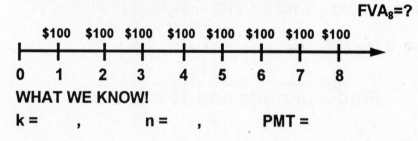

WHAT WE KNOW!

k =   ,   n =   ,   PMT =

Finding The Future Value Of An Annuity Due (FVAD$_n$)

5-29

Since each payment of an annuity due is received one period sooner, each is compounded for one year longer than for an ordinary annuity

Since our table is built for ordinary annuities, we need to make one simple adjustment to the formula to allow for the extra compounding period.

$$FVAD_n = PMT \times (FVIFA_{k,n}) \times (1 + k)$$

5-30

Example

A $100 annuity due for eight years at 7% annual interest would result in the following future value:

$$FVAD_8 = ?$$

$100 $100 $100 $100 $100 $100 $100 $100

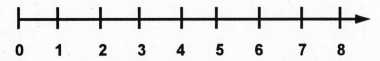

0   1   2   3   4   5   6   7   8

Other Uses Of The FVIFA Table: Example

5-31

How many annual deposits of $1,000 must be made to accumulate $7,500 in an account paying 9% annual compound interest?

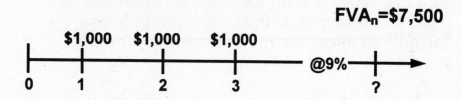

$$FVA_n = \$7,500$$

5-32

What we know

$$k = .09; \quad PMT = 1,000; \quad FVA_n = 7,500$$

Plug into the formula

$$7500 = 1,000 (FVIFA_{.09,n}) (1.09)$$

5-33   *Finding the k: Example*

Dave Carson can afford to put $2,500/year in an account for the next 15 years. If he wishes to have $100,000 at the end of that time, what is the minimum rate of return the account must have?

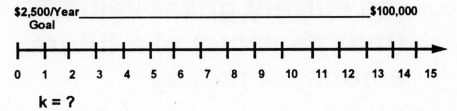

$2,500/Year
Goal $100,000

k = ?

5-34   *What we know*

$FVA_{15} =$; PMT =   0; n =

Plug into the formula

Present Value of a Single Amount

5-35

The Concept of Present Value:

Present Value concerns the current dollar value (today's value) of a future amount of money

5-36   ## *Present Value Formula*

$$PV = FVn \left(\frac{1}{1 + k} \right)^{n}$$

$$= FV_n \times (PVIF_{k,n})$$

PVIF factors are found in Table A-3

A Graphic View of Present Value

5-37

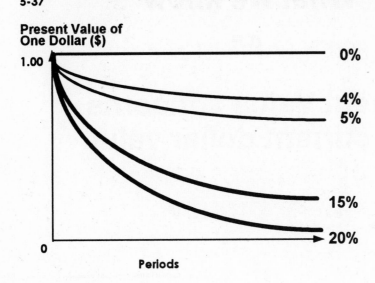

Present Value of One Dollar ($)

1.00

0%

4%

5%

15%

20%

0

Periods

5-38

Example

What is the present value of $1,000 due to be received four years from today assuming that if you had the dollar equivalent today, you could invest it at 8%?

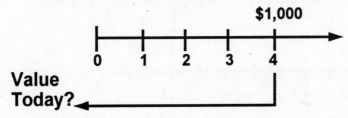

$1,000

0   1   2   3   4

Value Today?

5-39
What we know

$FV_4 =$; $n =$, $k =$

5-40
Example

What is the most you would pay for an opportunity to receive $10,000 at the end of 10 years if you can earn 9% on similar investments?

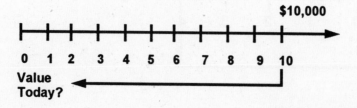

5-41
Example

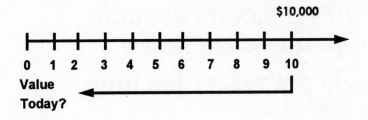

$10,000

0 1 2 3 4 5 6 7 8 9 10

Value
Today?

PV =

5-42
You Try One

What is the value today of $1,000 to be received in five years for a person with an opportunity cost of 11%?

WHAT WE KNOW!

$FV_5 =$; $n =$; $k = \%$

Important notes regarding the PVIF tables

5-43

- The $PVIF_{k,n}$ factors assume end-of-period cash flows
- $PVIF_{k,n}$ is always <1 (as long as k > o)
- As k ↑ , the $PVIF_{k,n}$ also ↓
- As n ↑ , the $PVIF_{k,n}$ also ↓

5-44 ## Comparing Present Value and Future Value

The values in the PVIF Tables are the inverse, or reciprocal, values of those in the FVIF tables for the same interest rate and number of periods

5-45   *Example*

FVIF$_{7\%,7}$ = 1.606
If we take the reciprocal

$$\frac{1}{1.606} = .623$$

Which is the factor for PVIF$_{7\%,7}$

5-46   *Other Uses Of The PVIF Table*

Finding the k is exactly like finding the k using the FVIF Table

5-47
Example

At what rate of interest would you be indifferent between $650 today and $1,000 in five years?

• WHAT WE KNOW!

PV =   ; FV_5 =   ;   n =
Plug into formula

5-48
Other Uses Of The PVIF Table

• **Finding the n is also the same except, due to the inverse relationship of the tables, you must find a table factor ≤ to the algebraic solution to the problem**

5-49   *Example*

After how many periods would you be indifferent between having $1,000 today or $1,200 in the future assuming you can earn 6% on your investments today?

5-50   *Example*

WHAT WE KNOW!

PV =   ; FV$_n$ =   ; k =

Plug into the formula

5-51

Present Value of Cash Flow Streams

Present Value Of A Mixed Stream

Mixed streams are non-annuity cash flows, i.e. they reflect no particular pattern

5-52

Example

Given the following mixed stream of cash flows for the next four years and a discount rate of 6%, what is the present value of the cash flow stream?

Year	Cash Flow
1	100
2	400
3	1,000
4	300

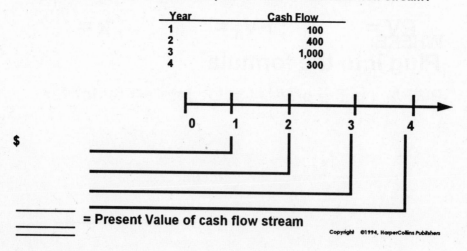

\$

_____ = Present Value of cash flow stream

Copyright ©1994, HarperCollins Publishers

5-53   *Present Value of An Annuity*

Annuity streams are, once again, equally sized and spaced

- **The present value of an annuity is the lump-sum amount needed today to permit equal-sized and equal-spaced withdrawals for 'n' periods**

- **This is also the technique used to compute payments on installment loans**

5-54   *Basic formula:*

$$PVA_n = PMT \times (PVIFA_{k,n})$$

WHERE:

$PVIFA_{k,n}$ is the present-value interest factor for an annuity(Table A-4)

The values in the PVIFA table are an accumulation of the values from the PVIF table (Table A-3)

5-55

Example

The PV of a three-year annuity of $100 discounted at 6% can be found by discounting each cash flow by the appropriate PVIF

Value: Yr 1: $100 x (.943) = $
           Yr 2: $100 x (.890) =
           Yr 3: $100 x (.840) =

$ _____

5-56

Example

Margaret Taylor wants to have $4,000 at the beginning of each of her four years of college - starting one year from today. If she can earn 8% annually, how much does she need to deposit in the account today?

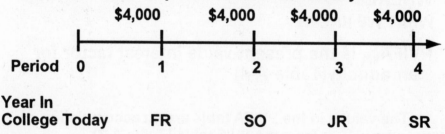

5-57   **What We Know**

PMT =   ;   k =   ;   n =
Plug into formula

5-58   *Example*

**What's the most you would pay today to purchase a
$5,000 15-year ordinary annuity given you can earn
12% annual interest on similar-risk investments?**

WHAT WE KNOW!
PMT =   ;   k =   ;   n =

Plug into formula

5-59   *If you have an annuity due, adjust the formula as follows:*

$$PVAD_n = PMT \times (PVIFA_{k,n}) \times (1 + k)$$

Note that the PV of an annuity due will be greater than that of an ordinary annuity of the same size and duration. Because the payments occur sooner, they are worth more.

5-60   *Example*

If Margaret Taylor was starting college *today* and still wanted $4,000 per year, we can compute the PV of her annuity as:
(Recall that k = 8%)

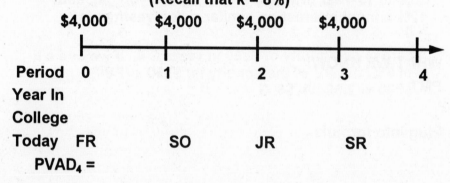

Period   0   1   2   3   4

Year In College

Today   FR   SO   JR   SR

$PVAD_4 =$

Present Value Of A Mixed Stream With An Embedded Annuity

5-61

- **If a Mixed Stream has an annuity embedded within it, the present value calculation can be simplified by determining the present value of the annuity first, and then discounting it back to time zero as a lump sum**

5-62

Example

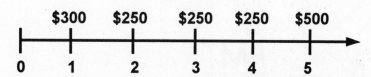

There is an annuity of \$250 in years 2-4. If we use a k of 7%, the PV of the annuity is: \$250 x (PVIFA$_{7\%,3}$) = \$250 x (2.624) = \$656

This amount corresponds to the beginning of year 2, which is the end of year 1. Thus, the lump sum (\$656) must be discounted one more year to time zero. This is simplified by adding the \$656 to the \$300 year 1 cash flow and discounting the combined amount.

5-63   *Example*

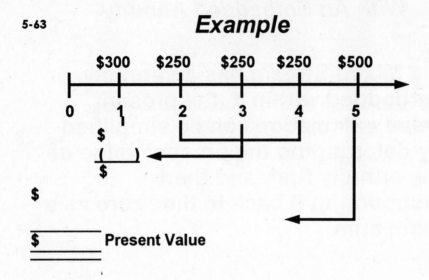

$ _____ **Present Value**

5-64   *Present Value Of A Perpetuity*

$$PVA_\infty = \frac{PMT}{k}$$

$$\text{Where } PVIFA_{k,\infty} = \frac{1}{k}$$

Example

5-65

If you wanted to endow a Finance scholarship of $1,000 per year forever, given that the University will always earn 5% on such deposits, how large a deposit would you have to make?

k =   ; PMT =   ; n =

Special Applications of Time Value

5-66

• Deposits to Accumulate a Future Sum

  • A common application of time value is to determine the annual deposit required to accumulate a particular sum of money at a particular time in the future.

5-67

Example

How much would you have to deposit annually at the end
of each of the next five years into an account paying
8% annual interest in order to accumulate $20,000
needed for a down payment on a new home?

WHAT WE KNOW!

$FVA_5 =$; k =   ; n =

5-68

Loan Amortization

Loan Amortization

**Definition: The determination of the
equal annual (periodic) loan
payments necessary to provide a
lender with a specified interest return
and repay the loan principal over a
specified period.**

Example

5-69

How much would your annual end-of-year payments
have to be on a $12,000 loan with a 15% interest rate
that must be fully repaid in three years?

WHAT WE KNOW!

$PVA_3 =$ $; k =$ $; n =$

Example

5-70

End of Year	Loan Payment (1)	Beginning of Year Principal (2)	Payments Interest [.15 x (2)] (3)	Payments Principal [(1)-(3)] (4)	End-of-Year Principal [(2)-(4)] (5)
1	$5,256.24	$12,000.00	$1,800.00	$3,456.24	$8,543.76
2	5,256.24	8,543.76	1,281.56	3,974.68	4,569.08
3	5,254.24	4,569.08	685.36	4,569.08	0
Total	$15,766.92		$3,766.92	$12,000.00	

Interest or Growth Rates: Example

5-71

What rate of growth in EPS did the firm experience between 1989 and 1994 given the following data?

Year	EPS	
1994	$5.80	} Treat as FV
1993	5.50	
1992	5.00	} Ignore Incremental
1991	4.75	Changes
1990	4.15	
1989	3.75	} Treat as PV

Interest or Growth Rates: Example

5-72

Using PV Techniques

$$PV = FV_n \; X \; PVIF_{k,n}$$

$$PV/FV_n = PVIF_{k,5} =$$

From table A-3: $PVIF_{9\%,5} =$
$PVIF_{10\%,5} =$
$$FV_5 = PV \; X \; (PVIF_{k,n})$$
$$FV_5/PV = FVIF_{k,5} =$$
From Table A-1: $FVIF_{.9\%,3} =$

Example

5-73

What's the approximate interest rate being paid on a $7,000 loan requiring equal annual payments of $1,700 at the end of each year over six years?

$k =$; PMT =   ; $PVA_6 =$; $n =$

Other Manipulations Of Time Value Problems: Example

5-74

Given the time line below, determine the present value of the cash flows at a discount rate of 12%

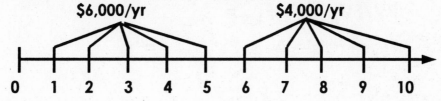

$6,000/yr $4,000/yr

0   1   2   3   4   5   6   7   8   9   10

Other Manipulations Of Time Value Problems: Example

5-75

Solution 1

Other Manipulations Of Time Value Problems: Example

5-76

Solution 2

Other Manipulations Of Time Value Problems: Example

5-77

Solution 3

Other Manipulations Of Time Value Problems: Example

5-78

The cumulative nature of the time value tables allows for the manipulation of table values to simplify further certain kinds of time value problems.

Choosing which Table to Use

5-79

Single payment problems use the PVIF of FVIF Tables

For annuity problems it is helpful to draw the time line and determine where the lump sum occurs

5-80

Example

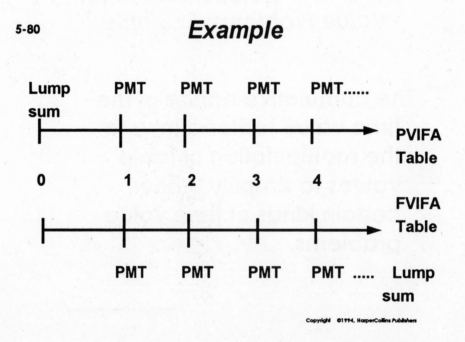

5-81   ## DISCUSSION PROBLEM

Linda Cooper has won first prize in her sorority raffle. She has a choice of receiving $100 today, or $150 in two years when she graduates. Which choice should Linda make if she can earn 20% on her money today?

Choice 1: $100 today
Choice 2: $150, two years from today

5-82   ## SOLUTION

5-83 ### *DISCUSSION PROBLEM*

Tom Johnson borrowed $50,000 to purchase a condo. The terms were 12% annual interest to be repaid in equal annual installments over 25 years, with the first payment due one year from today. What is the size of his annual payment?

_____

5-84 ### *DISCUSSION PROBLEM*

Warren Reed just turned 40. He has decided that he would like to retire when he is 65. He thinks that he will need $1,500,000 in his special retirement account at age 65 to maintain his current lifestyle. For the next 15 years he can afford to put $12,000 per year into the account. At age 55 he will need to withdraw $40,000 to purchase membership in the local country club. If his retirement account earns 11% compounded annually, how much will Warren need to deposit into it each year for the last ten years of his work career to attain the $1,500,000 goal?

DISCUSSION PROBLEM

5-85

Draw a Time Line

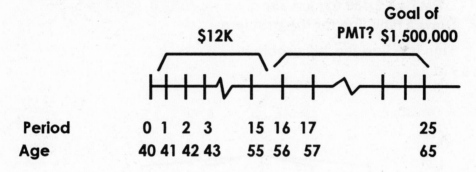

Period	0	1	2	3		15	16	17		25
Age	40	41	42	43		55	56	57		65

5-86

DISCUSSION PROBLEM

Determine how much Warren's account will be worth at age 65

What we Know:

PMT =   ; k =   ; n =

PV_A =

DISCUSSION PROBLEM

**Suppose you know the following data: PVA = $10,000;
PMT = $2,439.02; k = 7%**

Draw a time line for the problem

This is a find the "n" problem

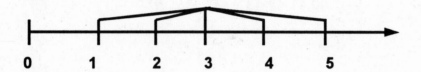

$$0 \quad 1 \quad 2 \quad 3 \quad 4 \quad 5$$

6-1

Risk and Return

Risk And Return Fundamentals

Basic Risk Concepts: A Single Asset

Risk Of A Portfolio

International Diversification

Risk and Return: The Capital Asset Pricing Model (CAPM)

Risk and Return Fundamentals

6-2

Introduction

The key determinants of share price are risk and return and all financial decisions must be evaluated in terms of expected risk and expected return

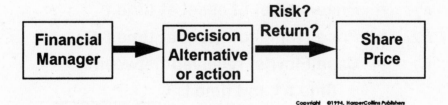

Copyright ©1994, HarperCollins Publishers

Risk and Return Defined

6-3

■**Risk is the chance of loss; the variability of returns; uncertainty associated with a given asset**

■**Return is the total gain or loss experienced by the owner of a financial asset or investment over a given period of time**

(6-4) *Return can be computed (ex post) or estimated (ex ante)*

$$k_t = \frac{P_t - P_{t-1} + C_t}{P_{t-1}}$$

WHERE

k_t = Actual (ex post) or expected (ex ante) return

P_t = Price (value) of asset at time *t*

P_{t-1} = Price (value) of asset at time *t*-1

C_t = Cash Flow(s) received between time *t*-1 and time t

Copyright ©1994, HarperCollins Publishers

6-5

Example

Reed Landers bought a share of Torbert Company stock
one year ago for $40. Today it can be sold for $43.50.
Reed received $1.50 in dividends during the year.
What is Reed's actual return for the year?

What We Know

$P_t = \$43.50$; $P_{t-1} = \$40.00$; $C_t = \$1.50$

Plug into formula

$$K_t = \frac{\$43.50 - \$40.00 + \$1.50}{\$40.00} = \frac{\$5.00}{\$40.00} = 12.5\%$$

6-6

Risk Preferences

• Risk-Indifferent

• Risk-Averse

• Risk-Seeking

Most managers are risk-averse and require higher returns for increasing risks

Risk Preferences

6-7

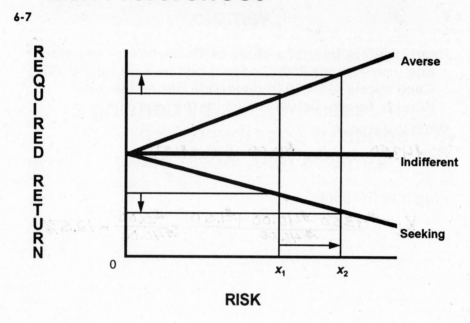

Basic Risk Concepts: A Single Asset

6-8

Risk of a Single Asset

While most investors or financial managers are unlikely to "put all their eggs in one basket," a single asset held in isolation provides an opportunity to study important risk and return relationships

Sensitivity Analysis

6-9

Sensitivity Analysis is a method of assessing risk by deriving a series of possible return estimates (e.g. worst case, most likely case, best case) to obtain a sense of the variability among outcomes

Example

6-10

- **Asset A and Asset B each require an initial investment of $10,000. They each have an expected annual return of 12% but differ greatly in their ranges of possible outcomes, as shown in the table:**

	Asset A	Asset B
Initial investment	$10,000	$10,000
Annual rate of return		
Worst case (pessimistic)	8%	3%
Most likely case (expected)	12%	12%
Best case (optimistic)	15%	19%
Range (Best-Worst cases)	7%	16%

6-11   *Probabilities*

■Probabilities are the percentage chances of given outcomes actually occurring

■An outcome with a probability of 100 percent is certain to occur while an outcome with a probability of zero percent will never occur

6-12   *Probability Distributions*

• Probability Distributions are schematic models that relate probabilities to associated outcomes

  »A Bar Chart shows a limited number of probability -outcome coordinates

  »A Continuous Probability Distribution shows all the possible probability-outcome coordinates for a given event

Probability Distributions

6-13

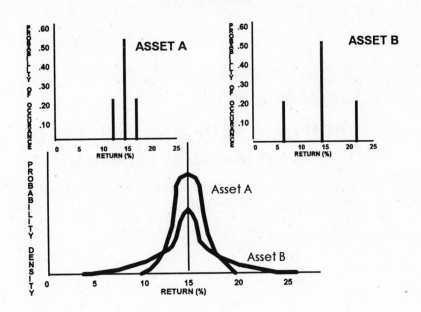

6-14 # *Standard Deviation*

**Standard Deviation is the
most common statistical
measure of an asset's risk;
it measures the absolute
variation or dispersion
around the expected (most
likely) return of the asset**

The smaller the SD, the less risk

Expected return ($\overline{k}$) is computed as follows:

6-15

$$\overline{k} = \sum_{i=1}^{n} k_i \times Pr_i$$

Where:

k_i = Return for the ith outcome

Pr_i = Probability of the ith outcome's occurance

n = Number of outcomes considered

Standard deviation (σ_k) is computed as follows:

6-16

$$\sigma_k = \sqrt{\sum_{i=1}^{n} (k_i - \overline{k})^2 \times Pr_i}$$

In general, the higher the standard deviation, the greater the risk

Example

(6-17)

A certain asset will return 28% if the economy takes off, 12% if the economy remains stable, and -15% if the economy goes into a recession. The latest economic projections show a 10% chance of the market taking off, a 75% chance of market stability, and a 15% chance of a recession.

Calculate expected return (weighted average return)

(6-18)

Outcome (i)	Pr_i	k_i	$Pr_i \times k_i$
Take off	.10	.28	.0280
Stability	.75	.12	.0900
Recession	.15	-.15	-.0225
	1.00		.0955

or <u>9.55%</u>

Calculate the standard deviation

Outcome (i)	Pr_i	k_i	$\bar{k}$	$(k_i - \bar{k})$	$(k_i - \bar{k})^2$	x	Pr_i
Take Off	.10	.28	.0955	.1845	.0340	x .10	= .0034
Stability	.75	.12	.0955	.0245	.0006	x .75	= .0005
Recession	.15	-.15	.0955	-.2455	.0603	x .15	= .0090

Variance (σ_k^2) = .0129

$$\sigma_k = \sqrt{.0129} \qquad = \underline{.1136 \ or \ 11.36\%}$$

-13%   32%

-2%   9.55%   21%

$\sigma = 11.36\%$

1 SD = 68% = less risk
2 SD = 95%
3 SD = 99%

Coefficient of Variation

Coefficient of variation is a measure of relative
variability useful for comparing two or more
assets with differing expected returns

Coefficient of Variation (CV) is computed as
follows:

$$CV = \frac{\sigma_k}{\bar{k}}$$

The higher the coefficient of variation, the
greater the risk

Example

(6-21)

Les Harrison is trying to determine which of the following two assets is more risky. Asset one has a k of 8% and a σ_k of 7%. Asset two has a k of 15% and a σ_k of 12%. Let's see if the coefficient of variation helps Les decide.

$$CV_{one} = \frac{.07}{.08} = .875$$

$$CV_{two} = \frac{.12}{.15} = .800$$

Thus, asset one is slightly more risky.

6-22   ## *Risk and Time*

Risk is an increasing function of time due to greater uncertainty caused by increased forecasting errors for distant years

Thus, the longer-lived an asset investment, the greater its risk

(6-23)   # *Risk of a Portfolio*

A *portfolio* is a collection of assets

An *efficient portfolio* is a collection of assets managed to either maximize return for a given level of risk or minimize risk for a given level of return

6-24   ## *Portfolio Return and Standard Deviation*

To compute the return of a portfolio you must use the weighted average of the returns of all assets in the portfolio, with the weight given each asset calculated as:

$$\frac{\text{Dollar value of each asset}}{\text{Total dollar value of the portfolio}}$$

The portfolio return (k_p) is found by the formula

$$k_p = (w_1 \times k_1) + (w_2 + k_2) + ... (w_n \times k_n) = \sum_{j=1}^{n} w_j \times k_j$$

WHERE:

w_j = weight of asset j
k_j = return on asset j

Correlation

(6-25)

Correlation is a statistical measure of the relationship between two series of numbers

Positively Correlated means the series move in the same direction

Negatively Correlated means the series move in opposite directions

Correlation Coefficient is a measure of the strength of relationship between two series

- A correlation coefficient of *+1 indicates perfect positive correlation*

-1 indicates perfect negative correlation

0 indicates uncorrelated

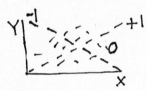

Diversification

(6-26)

Diversification is a method of reducing the risk of a portfolio by combining assets that have negative (or low positive) correlation
Combinations of assets that are:

1. Negatively Correlated can reduce σ_k below that of the least risky asset

2. Uncorrelated can reduce σ_k, below that of the least risky asset, but not as effectively as with negatively correlated assets

3. Positively Correlated can reduce σ_k below that of the least risky asset but not as effectively as with uncontrolled assets

Diversification

(6-27)

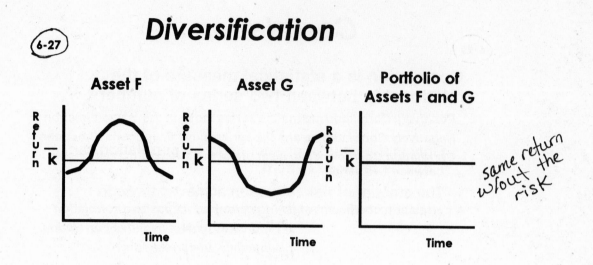

Asset F   Asset G   Portfolio of Assets F and G

same return w/out the risk

Portfolio Return and Portfolio Risk

6-28

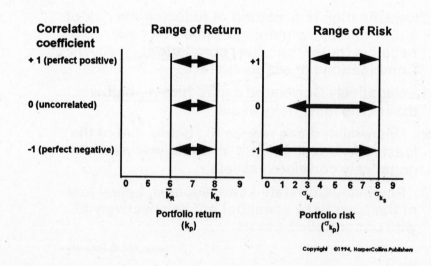

Correlation, Diversification, Risk, and Return

In general, the lower the correlation between asset returns, the greater the potential diversification of risk

Only in the case of perfect negative correlation can risk be reduced to zero

The amount of risk reduction achieved through diversification is also dependent upon the proportions in which the assets are combined

There is potentially an infinite number of asset combinations possible in a given portfolio of assets

Types of Risk

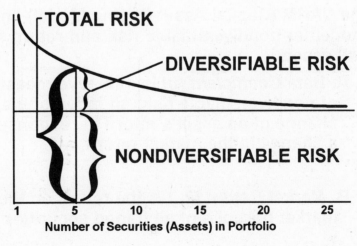

standard deviation of returns for the stock market as a whole.

(6-31) ### *The Capital Asset Pricing Model (CAPM)*

Types of Risk

The total risk of a financial asset is made up of two components

A. Diversifiable (unsystematic) risk

B. Nondiversifiable (systematic) risk

The only relevant risk is nondiversifiable risk, and its measurement is of extreme importance in selecting assets with the most desired risk-return characteristics

The Model: CAPM

(6-32)

The CAPM (Capital Asset Pricing Model) links together nondiversifiable risk and return for all assets

A. *Beta Coefficient (b)* is a relative measure of nondiversifiable risk; an index of the change of an asset's return in response to a change in the market return $= 1$

B. *Market Return (k$_m$)* is the return on the market portfolio of all traded securities

The Model: CAPM

(6-33)

C. Market Beta = 1.0 = average level of risk
1. A Beta of .5 is half as risky as average
2. A Beta of 2.0 is twice as risky as average
3. A negative Beta asset moves in opposite direction to market

D. Beta Coefficients are easily obtained from published sources, such as *Value Line Investment Survey*, and through brokerage firms

E. Portfolio Betas are determined by calculating the weighted average of the Betas of all assets included in the portfolio, using each asset's proportion of the total dollar value of the portfolio as its weight

The equation for the CAPM is:

(6-34)

not given on tes

$$k_j = R_F + [b_j \times (k_m - R_F)]$$

given on test

WHERE:

k_j = Required return on asset j;

R_F = Risk-free rate of return

b_j = Beta Coefficient for asset j;

k_m = Market return

and

The term $[b_j \times (k_m - R_F)]$ is called the risk premium and $(k_m - R_F)$ is called the market risk premium

Example

6-35

Given a risk-free rate of 5% and a market return of 10%, what is the required return for stock j with a Beta of 1.5?

$$k_j = $$
$$= $$
$$= $$
$$= \underline{\qquad\qquad} \%$$

The graphic depiction of CAPM:

(6-36)

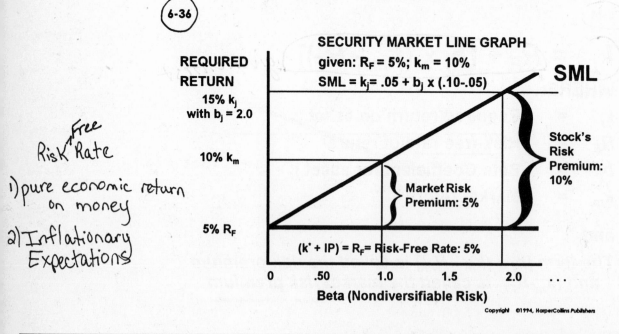

SECURITY MARKET LINE GRAPH

given: R_F = 5%; k_m = 10%

SML = k_j = .05 + b_j x (.10-.05)

SML

REQUIRED RETURN

15% k_j with b_j = 2.0

10% k_m

5% R_F

Stock's Risk Premium: 10%

Market Risk Premium: 5%

(k^* + IP) = R_F = Risk-Free Rate: 5%

| 0 | .50 | 1.0 | 1.5 | 2.0 | . . . |

Beta (Nondiversifiable Risk)

Free
Risk Rate

1) pure economic return on money

2) Inflationary Expectations

Shifts in the Security Market Line

6-37

What if?

- Inflation increases or decreases?

- Investors become more, or less, risk-averse?

- A security temporarily is not "on" the security market line?

Security Market Line

6-38

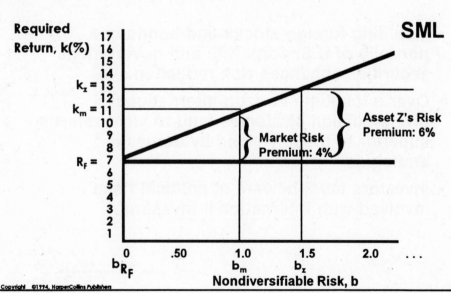

6-39 *Some Comments on CAPM*

- **Since Beta coefficients are derived from historical data, they are best viewed as approximations of future expectations of actual risk-return behaviors**

- **CAPM is based upon an assumed efficient market which, although seemingly unrealistic, is supported empirically in active markets such as the New York Stock Exchange**

- **While CAPM is not applicable to all assets, it does provide a conceptual framework that is useful in linking risk and return in financial decisions**

International Diversification

6-40

- **Including foreign stocks and bonds in a portfolio of U.S. corporate and government securities enhances risk reduction.**

- **Over a longtime horizon international diversification strategies tend to yield returns superior to those yielded by domestic strategies**

- **Investors must beware of political risks involved with international investing.**

DISCUSSION PROBLEM

6-41

Ben Lewis has found the following data relative to the stock of the Spivey Corporation and current conditions:

Required/expected return   = 20%

Market portfolio return   = 11%

Risk premium for market portfolio = 6%

What is the Beta of the Spivey Corporation stock?

6-42   *Determine the risk-free rate*

Algebraic Solution   **Graphic Solution**

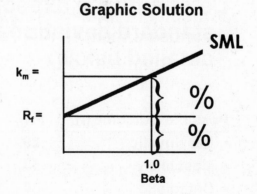

6-43   *Plug into SML formula*

DISCUSSION PROBLEM

6-44

Determine the expected return and standard deviation for the asset detailed below:

Possible Outcome (i)	Pr($_i$)	Return (k_i)
• Pessimistic	.20	.14
• Most likely	.50	.16
• Optimistic	.30	.18

DISCUSSION PROBLEM

6-45

A.   **Expected return (k):**

    $(Pr_j \times k_j)$

B.   **Standard Deviation (σ_k):**

7-1   *Valuation*

- **Valuation Fundamentals**
- **Bond Valuation**
- **Common Stock Valuation**
- **Decision Making And Common Stock Value**

7-2   *Valuation Fundamentals*

•Valuation is the process of determining the worth of an asset through the linking of risk and return

7-3   *Valuation Fundamentals*

Since financial assets represent claims on the future cash flows of their issuers, their valuation must take into consideration the size and number of cash flows to be received, the timing of the cash flows, and the required return (risk) of the investor

7-4   *Valuation Fundamentals*

•Cash flows (returns)
•Timing
•Required return (risk)

(7-5)

The Basic Valuation Model

$$V_o = \frac{CF_1}{(1+k)^1} + \frac{CF_2}{(1+k)^2} + \ldots + \frac{CF_n}{(1+k)^n}$$

WHERE:

V_o = value of the asset at time zero (today)

CF_t = cash flow expected at the end of the year t

k = appropriate required return (discount rate)

n = relevant time period

7-6

The Basic Valuation Model

The basic valuation equation can be rewritten in terms of present-value notation as follows:

$$V_o = [CF_1 \times (PVIF_{k,1})] + [CF_2 \times (PVIF_{k,2})] + \ldots + [CF_n \times (PVIF_{k,n})]$$

7-7   *Example*

**Stan Stockton inherited some stock at age 18 with the stipulation
that he cannot sell it until he is 21. He has learned that the stock
will pay him $100 at the end of each year while he owns it and that
it will have a market value of $1,000 when he is able to sell it. If
Stan has a required rate of return of 8%, what is the value of the
stock today?**

Draw a time line to visualize the problem $1,000

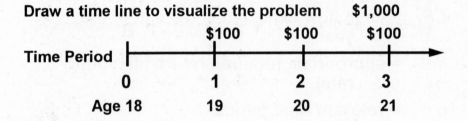

7-8   *Example*

(7-9) *Bond Valuation*

Bond valuation is easily performed since bond interest is paid in annuity form and bonds mature at a specified time, returning a known amount at maturity (i.e. cash flows and timing are known)

(7-10) *Bond Fundamentals*

Bond A long term debt, sold or issued by corporation

Par Value Legal stated value

Coupon Interest Rate % of par that the bond pays in interest on an ~~avg~~ annual basis

Interest payment paid in cash usually semiannually

Bond prices what investors are willing to pay (market price)

"quoted" A % of the par value of the bond

Current yield Its annual interest payment ÷ current market price

Interest rate risk The fluctuation in market price of bond due to changes interest rate. The longer the bond has to mature the greater the interest rate risk.

Copyright 1994, HarperCollins Publishers

7-11   *Bond Fundamentals*

A $1,000 par value bond quoted at 96 has a price of $960

A $1,000 par value bond quoted at 102 $\frac{1}{2}$ has a price of $1,025

7-12   *Example*

Given a $1,000 par value bond with a 10% coupon rate, currently quoted at 96, the current yield is

$$\underline{\hspace{5cm}} = \underline{\hspace{2cm}}$$

7-13 **Bond Fundamentals**

Selling at a *discount* is when a bond sells for less than its par value (i.e., the quote is <100)

Selling at *premium* is when a bond sells for more than its par value (i.e., the quote is >100)

7-14 **Basic Bond Valuation**

$$B_o = I \times (PVIFA_{k_d,n}) + M \times (PVIF_{k_d,n})$$

WHERE:

B_o = value of the bond at time zero

I = annual bond interest in dollars (interest payment)

M = par value of the bond

k_d = required rate of return

n = number of years to maturity

7-15
Example

A $1,000 par value bond matures in 20 years and has a
9% coupon interest rate. If an investor's required
rate of return is 10%, what is the value of the bond?

What We Know:

$M = \$1,000$; $I = .09 \times 1,000 = \$90$; $n = 20$; $k_d = 10\%$

$B_0 = \$90 \times (PVIFA_{10\%, 20}) + 1,000 (PVIF_{10\%, 20})$

$\quad = \$90 \times (8.514) + \$1,000 \times (.149)$

$\quad = \$766.16 + \$149$

$\quad = \$915.26$

Thus, the most an investor w/a 10% required
return would pay for this bond is $915.26,
or a quote of approximately 91½.

7-16
Example

What if another investor's required return on
the same bond is only 9%

$B_0 =$

NOTE: Bond value will always equal par
value (except for a small rounding error)
when the required return is equal to the
coupon rate

7-17

Bond Value Behavior

- Bond values normally fluctuate over their lives due to external forces changes in the firm's risk, and the passage of time

- If the required rate of return is not equal to the coupon rate, then the bond's value will not be equal to its par value

7-18   *Example*

- After the divestiture of AT&T analysts lowered the corporation's bond rating due to the uncertainty of the outcome of the massive breakup. While AT&T eventually regained its former top rating, for the interim period their cost of debt was higher as a result of investors increasing their required rates of return on AT&T bonds

7-19

Yield To Maturity (YTM)

- **YTM is the rate of return investors earn if they buy a bond at a specific price and hold it until maturity**
- **YTM is also the discount rate that causes the bond's current price to just equal the present value of its interest payments and par value**
- **There are three basic methods of determining YTM**
  - ✗ **Trial and error**
  - ② **Approximation formula**
  - ✗ **Use of a business/financial calculator**

7-20   *Example*

A $1,000 bond paying 12% annual (coupon) interest will mature in 8 years. Its current price is $1,060. Determine its YTM.

Trial and Error

Bo   =

7-21   *Example*

7-22   *Example*

To interpolate:

7-23

Example

Approximation Formula $YTM =$

$$\frac{I + \left(\dfrac{M - B_0}{n}\right)}{\dfrac{M + B_0}{2}} = \frac{\$120 + \left(\dfrac{\$1{,}000 - \$1{,}060}{8}\right)}{\dfrac{\$1{,}000 + \$1{,}060}{2}}$$

$$= \frac{\$112.5}{\$1030} = \underline{10.992\ \%}$$

 ## *Semiannual Interest and Bond Values*

Since most bonds pay interest every six months, it increases the present value of the cash flows and, thus, the value of the bond

Adjust the valuation formula as follows:

$$B_0 = I/2 \ x \left(PVIFA_{\frac{k_d}{2},\,2xn}\right) + M \ x \left(PVIF_{\frac{k_d}{2},\,2xn}\right)$$

(7-25)

Example

A $1,000 par bond with a 15% coupon and 15 years to maturity and semiannual interest payments is being considered by an investor with a 10% required return. How much should he be willing to pay?

$$B_0 = \$150/2 \times \left(PVIFA_{\frac{10}{2}, 2\times15} \right) + \$1,000 \times \left(PVIF_{\frac{10}{2}, 2\times15} \right)$$

$$= \$75 \times \left(PVIFA_{5\%, 30} \right) + \$1,000 \times \left(PVIF_{5\%, 30} \right)$$

$$= \$75 \left(15.373 \right) + \$1,000 \left(.231 \right)$$

$$= \$1,383.98$$

9/8

Preferred Stock
→Equity in the form of debt
 - Receive dividends
Adv. 1- Dividend must be paid for current & past years
       before common stockholders get anything

(7-26)   # *Common Stock Valuation*

2- In case of liquidation they have right to receive par value before common get anything

Disadv.:
1- Dividend is fixed in dollars per share or % of par value

• **Common stock valuation provides more challenge than bond valuation since common stock does not have:**

  – A maturity date

  – A stated liquidation value

  – Guaranteed dividends or dividend growth

  – Guaranteed price appreciation

Common Stock Valuation

– To find the value of common stock, assumptions must be made regarding the growth of dividends and/or price

» These assumptions allow the investor to estimate the benefits to be received from the stock over the relevant time period

» The estimated benefits are then used to calculate expected return ($\hat{k}$)

$$\hat{k} = \frac{\textit{Expected Benefits During Each Period}}{\textit{Current Price of Asset}}$$

Perpituity = A security that pays the same payment into infinity

Go To Notes

Market Efficiency

- **Efficient market**
- **Equilibrium price**
- **Basic decision rules:**
  – If $\hat{k}$ is less than k (required return), the asset will not be purchased
  – If $\hat{k}$ is equal to or greater than k, the asset will be purchased
  – Price adjustments occur whenever $\hat{k} \neq k$

(7-29) **Basic Stock Valuation Equation**

The value of a share of stock is equal to the present value of all future dividends

Key symbols and terminology

P_o = value of common stock today

D_t = per-share dividend expected in year t   *hope it will be higher in future years*

k_s = required return on stock

g = growth rate expected

7-30   *General formula:*

$$P_o = \frac{D_1}{(1+k_s)^1} + \frac{D_2}{(1+k_s)^2} + \ldots + \frac{D^\infty}{(1+k_s)^\infty}$$

(7-31)

General formula:

$$P_o = \frac{D_1}{(1+k_s)^1} + \frac{D_2}{(1+k_s)^2} + \ldots + \frac{D^\infty}{(1+k_s)^\infty}$$

There are three valuation models
Zero Growth Model (Naive Valuation)

Assumption: Constant, non-growing
dividend stream

Formula:

$$P_o = \frac{D_1}{k_s}$$

7-32

Example

Spivey Corporation stock will pay a dividend
of $2.12 next year. If Earl E. Byrd requires a
12% return and believes in naive valuation,
how much should he be willing to pay for a
share of Spivey stock?

$$P_o = \frac{\$2.12}{.12} = \$17.67$$

– NOTE: The zero growth model treats the stock as a
perpetuity

– This formula can be used to find the value of
preferred stock

7-33

Constant Growth Model
(Gordon Model)

Div '84 $\cancel{#}$1
'94 $\cancel{#}2$ = .500
$\hookrightarrow$ *look on table*
g = 7%

Assumptions:

- Dividends will grow at a constant annual compound rate, g

- Investor's required return is greater than the growth rate ($k_s > g$)

Formula:

$$P_o = \frac{D_1}{k_s - g} = \frac{\$1}{.15 - .10} = \$20$$

$D_o = \$.91$

$D_1 = D_o(1 + g)$

$\hookrightarrow$ *Expected dividend for next year*

$K_s = \dfrac{D_1}{P_o} + g$

$K_s = \dfrac{\$1}{\$20} + .10$

 7-34

Example

If a stock paid $2.16 per share in dividends last year and has a historical dividend growth rate of 7% per year, how much would an investor requiring an 11% return be willing to pay for a share of stock?

$D_1 = \$2.16$

$$P_o = \frac{\$2.16}{.11 - .07} = \frac{\$2.16}{.04} = \$54$$

NOTE: Any P_t can be found with the formula $P_t = \dfrac{D_{t+1}}{k_s - g}$

7-35

Variable Growth

Assumption: Allows for changes in the growth rate of dividends

Procedure:

Let g_1 = growth rate during initial period

Let g_2 = growth rate after the initial period

1. Find the present value of all dividends during the initial growth period

2. Find the present value of the value of stock at the end of the initial growth period

3. Add the results of 1 + 2 to determine P_0

NOTE: A time line is extremely helpful on these problems!

7-36

Example

The Torbert Corporation paid $1.00/share in dividends last year. Due to a new product, Torbert's CEO expects dividends to grow at 12% for two years. At that time the competition will have copied the product and growth will drop to 6%. Given a required return of 11%, what is P_0?

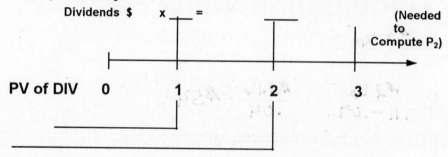

7-37   *Example*

2.

PV of P_2 =

3.

7-38 *Other Approaches to Common Stock Valuation*

•Book Value Per Share

•Liquidation Value Per Share

•Price/Earnings (P/E) Multiples

7-39 Decision Making and Stock Value

- **Valuation is based upon two types of variables**
  - **Expected return variables (D_1 and g)**
  - **Risk variable (k_s)**

7-40 Changes in Expected Return and Risk

- If management action results in either an increase in dividends or an increase in the dividend growth rate without increasing risk, the value of the firm's common stock should rise

- If management action results in an increase in risk for the firm, the required return of investors will also increase -resulting in a decrease in the value of a share of the firm's stock - and vice versa

7-41

Combined Effect

- **Management action most often affects both expected return variables and risk at the same time, thus the relative magnitude of the changes in these variables will determine if P_o will increase or decrease**

Extra Note on Common Stock Valuation

7-42

The amount of time an investor intends to hold a share of stock is irrelevant to the value of the stock to that investor.

Given: D_0 = $1.00;   g = 5%; k_s = 8%

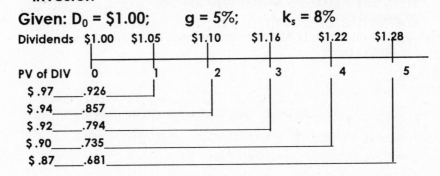

Extra Note on Common Stock Valuation

7-43

$P_o =$

$P_1 =$

$P_2 =$

$P_3 =$

$P_4 =$

$PV_1 =$

$PV_2 =$

$PV_3 =$

$PV_4 =$

7-44 ## DISCUSSION PROBLEMS

A. Ben Lewis is considering the purchase of a bond with the following characteristics:

– $1,000 par value

– 9% coupon interest rate, compounded annually

– 17 years to maturity

If Ben's required return is 8%, what is the most he should be willing to pay for the bond?

Bo =

7-45　　　**DISCUSSION PROBLEM**

B. If Ben purchased the bond for exactly the answer in (A) above, what would his yield-to-maturity be?

(Difference = PV of inflows - price)

7-46　　　**DISCUSSION PROBLEM**

Five years ago First-Quality Used Auto Corporation paid a dividend of $1.50 on its common stock. Today it paid a dividend of $2.10

A. What is the annual dividend growth rate, g?

B. Given the growth rate calculated in part (A), and a market required return of 11.5%, at what price should the stock be selling?

8-1   *Capital Budgeting and Cash Flow Principles*

- **The Capital Budgeting Decision Process**
- **The Relevant Cash Flows**
- **Finding the Initial Investment**
- **Finding The Operating Cash Inflows**
- **Finding the Terminal Cash Flow**
- **Summarizing The Relevant Cash Flows**

8-2   *The Capital Budgeting Decision Process*

- **Capital is funding**
- **Budget implies an expenditure plan**
- **Capital Budgeting is the process of evaluating and selecting long-term investments**

9/15

The Capital Budgeting Decision Process

(8-3)

- *Capital budgeting decisions are vital because*

    These assets represent relatively large expenditures of funds

    The funds are committed for lengthy periods of time

    It is both difficult and costly to reverse a capital budgeting decision

    Achievement of many of the firm's most important operational and financial goals is highly dependent upon capital investment decisions

(8-4)   *Capital Expenditure Motives*

- Motives for making capital expenditures :

    –**Expansion**: Amount of cash we need to invest in a project & how much comes back to us.

    –**Replacement**: Look at on investment & cash flow but also on an incremental basis

    –**Renewal**

    –**Other long-term outlays**
    Don't return a cash flow, so we relatively ignore it.

8-5   *Steps In The Process*

- **Proposal generation**
- **Review and analysis**
- **Decision making**
- **Implementation**
- **Follow-up**

(8-6)   *Basic Terminology*

- **Projects refers generally to any long-term investment proposals**
- **Independent Projects** – One which we may accept or reject on its own merits
- **Mutually Exclusive Projects** – If we buy one we don't buy the other
- **Unlimited Funds**
- **Capital Rationing** Limited pool of capital available in a given year.
- **Accept-Reject Approach**
- **Ranking Approach** All give positive return, but only have so much money, so we do the most important ones first.

8-7

Example

**A firm has funds available to fund only four projects from a group of
ten project proposals, A through J. All projects except those
noted as mutually exclusive are independent. Which four projects
should the firm implement given only the following data?**

Project		Rate of Return
A		13%
B		18%
C	Mutually Exclusive	16%
D		20%
E		17%
F		15%
G		19%
H	Mutually Exclusive	18%
I		22%
J		16%

8-8

Example

1. Determine best of mutually exclusive projects

**2. Then, rank remaining projects, including best of
mutually exclusive**

8-9   *Basic Terminology*

•Conventional Cash Flows

• Nonconventional Cash Flows

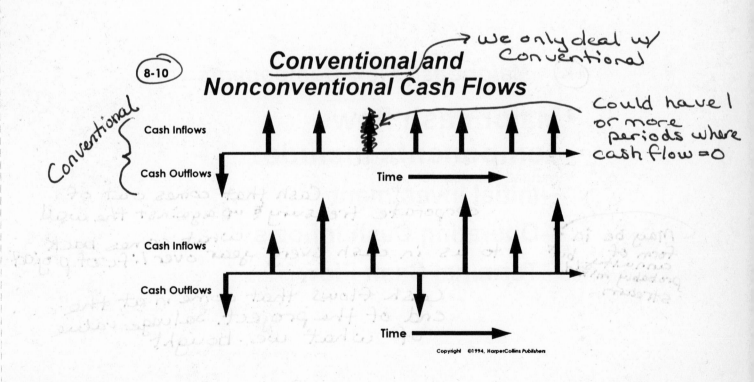

Conventional and
Nonconventional Cash Flows

we only deal w/ Conventional

Could have 1 or more periods where cash flow = 0

Conventional

Cash Inflows

Cash Outflows

Time

Cash Inflows

Cash Outflows

Time

8-11   *The Relevant Cash Flows*

- **Relevant Cash Flows include:**
  - **The incremental after-tax cash outflow (investment) for the project**
  - **The resulting subsequent cash inflows associated with the project**
- **Incremental Cash Flows are the additional cash flows directly attributable to the proposed project**

(8-12)   *Major Cash Flow Components*

- **Major cash flow components include:**
  - **Initial Investment** Cash that comes out of corporate treasury & up against the wall
  - **Operating Cash Inflows** what comes back to us in cash every year over life of project
  - **Terminal Cash Flow**

  Cash flows that come in at the end of the project. Salvage value of what we bought

  May be in form of annuity but probably mixed stream

(8-13)   *Cash Flow Components*

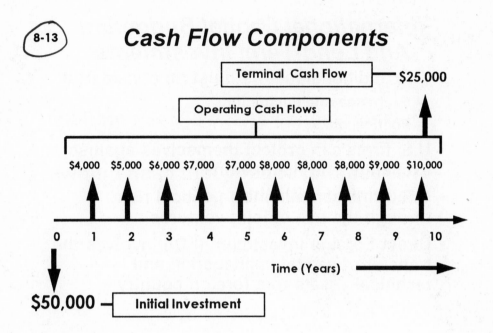

8-14   *Expansion Versus Replacement Cash Flows*

•Expansion decisions are straightforward

•Replacement decisions are more complicated

8-15 International Capital Budgeting And Long-Term Investments

- Two additional factors must be considered:
  - Exchange rate fluctuations
  - Political risks
- U.S. firms can protect themselves against exchange rate fluctuations
- U.S. firms can minimize political risk through the use of joint ventures
- Direct Foreign Investment (FDI) involves the transfer of capital, managerial, and technical assets to a foreign country

8-16 Finding the Initial Investment

- **The initial investment**
  - Initial investment is determined by subtracting all cash inflows occurring at time zero from all the cash outflows occurring at time zero
- **Installed Cost Of New Asset**
  - Outflows to be considered include:
    - »Cost of the new asset
    - »Installation costs

After-Tax Proceeds From Sale
Of Old Asset

(8-17)

(Replacement) • **Proceeds from sale of an old asset:** *Reduces cash flow for initial investment*

• **Taxes**

   – Book Value is the installed cost of the asset
      minus its accumulated depreciation

   – Four possible situations can arise:

   » sell the asset for more than its original
      purchase price *Capital Gain have to pay tax on Gain x tax rate*

   » sell the asset for more than its book value,
      but less than its original price *Have to pay tax on recaptured depreciation. Deprec.1 x tax rate*

   » sell the asset for its book value *Original Cost – Depreciation up to time of sale*

   » sell the asset for less than its book value

8-18   *Example*

An asset was originally purchased for $30,000 and now
   has a Book Value of $8,700. Assuming the firm has
   ordinary operating income during the period of sale,
   and a tax rate of 40%, compute the tax effects if the firm
   sells the asset at the following prices:

1.   Sale Price: $40,000

       Capital Gain   =

       Recaptured
       Depreciation   =   =
       Total Gain   =
       x Tax Rate   .40
       = Total Tax   =

8-19

Example

2. Sale Price: $20,000
Recaptured
Depreciation = =
x Tax Rate .40
= Total Tax =
(Added to Initial Investment)

3. Sale Price: $8,700

4. Sale Price: $5,000
Loss = =
x Tax Rate .40
= Tax Credit or Savings

8-20

Tax Treatment For Sale of Assets

FORM OF TAXABLE INCOME	DEFINITION	TAX TREATMENT	ASSUMED TAX RATE
Capital Gain	Sale Price in excess of initial purchase price	Total capital gain is taxed as ordinary income	40%
Recaptured deprecistion	Portion of the sale price that is in excess of book value and represents a recovery of previously taken depreciation	All recaptured depreciation is taxed as ordinary income	40%
Loss on Sale of asset	Amount by which the sale price is less than the book value	Depends on whether asset is depreciable	40% of loss is a tax savings

Copyright ©1994, HarperCollins Publishers

8-21   *Change in Net Working Capital*

▲If current assets will increase more than current liabilities, the result is an increase in net working capital which is treated as an initial outflow associated with the project

▲If the change in net working capital is negative, it is treated as an initial inflow associated with the project

Calculation of Change in Net Working Capital for Danson Company

8-22

Current account	Change in balance	
Cash	+ $ 4,000	
Accounts receivable	+ 10,000	
Inventories	+ 8,000	
(1) Current Assets		+22,000
Accounts payable	+ $ 7,000	
Accruals	+ 2,000	
(2) Current liabilities		+ 9,000
Change in net working capital [(1) - (2)]		+13,000

8-23

Example

The Torbert Company is considering the purchase of a new machine to replace an existing one. The existing machine was purchased three years ago at an installed cost of $25,000 and has been depreciated under MACRS using a five-year recovery period. The new machine will cost $30,000 and require a $5,000 installation cost. The existing machine can be sold for $17,500 with removal at the buyer's expense. Net working capital is expected to decrease $1,500 due to the replacement. Torbert's tax rate on both ordinary income and capital gains is 40%. Calculate the initial investment.

    1.   Isolate what we know we need:

Example

- 2.   **Determine tax effects on sale of old machine**

    a. Book Value of Old machine
$$= 25,000 - [(.20 + .32 + .19) \times 25,000]$$
$$= 7,250$$

    b. $17,500 - 7,250 = 10,250$
      (recaptured deprec.) $\times .40 = \$4,100$

- 3.   **Put it all together**

Cost of New machine	30,000
+ Installation costs	+ 5,000
– Proceeds from Old machine	– 17,500
+ Taxes on Sale of Old machine	+ 4,100
– Change in Net Working Capital	– 1,500
Initial Investment	$20,100

Finding the Operating Cash Inflows

8-25

- **Interpreting The Terms *After Tax*, *Cash Inflows*, And *Incremental***
- **The term "After-Tax" is important for 2 reasons:**
  - **Tax payments are cash outflows**
  - **It achieves consistency necessary for comparison to the initial investment**
- **The term *Cash Inflows* is important because:**
  - **It implies actual dollars that can be spent, not simply "accounting profits", which are not necessarily available for paying the obligations of the firm**

2nd Method

Tax Shield

$$EBDT \ (1-TR) = \$600$$
$$+ DEP. \ (TR) = 160$$
$$\overline{\quad CFAT \qquad \$760}$$

$1000 (.6)
$400 (.4)

TR = Tax Rate
EBDT = Earnings Before Deprec. & Taxes

Finding the Operating Cash Inflows 1st Method

8-26

- **The income statement format for calculating operating cash inflows is:**

	Revenue	$2000
-	Expenses (Excluding Depreciation)	1000
=	Profits Before Depreciation and Taxes	1000
-	Depreciation	400
=	Net Profits Before Taxes (Taxable Income)	600
-	Taxes 40%	240
=	Net Profits After Taxes	360
+	Depreciation	400
=	Operating Cash Inflows	$760

CFAT
(Cash Flow After Taxes)

8-27

Example

- Torbert Company's cost accountant has estimated that its revenues and expenses (excluding depreciation) are $28,000 and $7,800 respectively for each of the five years of usable life of the machine being considered (see example for initial investment). The old machine, which will last five years, elicits revenues of $15,000/year and expenses of $8,000/year. A depreciation schedule for the new machine and the existing machine follows:

Year	New Machine Cost	MACRS %	Depreciation
1	$35,000	20%	$ 7,000
2	$35,000	32%	11,200
3	$35,000	19%	6,650
4	$35,000	12%	4,200
5	$35,000	12%	4,200
6	$35,000	05%	1,750
		100%	$35,000

8-28

Example

Year	Old Machine Cost*	MACRS %	Depreciation
1	$25,000	12%	$ 3,000
2	$25,000	12%	3,000
3	$25,000	05%	1,250
4	-0-	---	-0-
5	-0-	---	-0-
6	-0-	---	-0-
		29%	$ 7,250

*Old machine has only three years of depreciable life remaining.

Calculation of Operating Cash Inflows for New and Existing Machine

8-29

New Machine	Year 1	Year 2	Year 3	Year 4	Year 5	Year 6
Revenue	$18,000	$18,000	$18,000	$18,000	$18,000	$ -0-
- Expenses (Excl. Depr.)	7,800	7,800	7,800	7,800	7,800	-0-
Profit Before Depr. & Taxes	$11,200	$11,200	$11,200	$11,200	$11,200	$ -0-
- Depreciation	7,000	11,200	6,650	4,200	4,200	1,750
Profit Before Taxes	$ 4,200	-0-	$ 4,550	$ 7,000	$ 7,000	$ (1,750)
- Taxes @ 40%	1,680	-0-	1,820	2,800	2,800	(700)
Net Profit	$ 2,520	-0-	$ 2,730	$ 4,200	$ 4,200	$ (1,050)
+ Depreciation	7,000	11,200	6,650	-0-	4,200	1,750
= Operating Cash Inflows	$ 9,520	$11,200	$ 9,380	$ 8,400	$ 8,400	$ 700
Existing Machine	**Year 1**	**Year 2**	**Year 3**	**Year 4**	**Year 5**	**Year 6**
Revenue	$15,000	$15,000	$15,000	$15,000	$15,000	$ -0-
- Expenses (Excel. Depr.)	8,000	8,000	8,000	8,000	8,000	-0-
Profit Before Depr. & Taxes	$ 7,000	$ 7,000	$ 7,000	$ 7,000	$ 7,000	$ -0-
- Depreciation	3,000	3,000	1,250	-0-	-0-	-0-
Profit Before Taxes	$ 4,000	$ 4,000	$ 5,750	$ 7,000	$ 7,000	
- Taxes @ 40%	1,600	1,600	2,300	2,800	2,800	-0-
Net Profit	$ 2,400	$ 2,400	$ 3,450	$ 4,200	$ 4,200	$ -0-
+ Depreciation	3,000	3,000	1,250	-0-	-0-	-0-
= Operating Cash Inflows	$ 5,400	$ 5,400	$ 4,700	$ 4,200	$ 4,200	$ -0-

Incremental Operating Cash Inflows for the Torbert Company

8-30

	NEW	EXISTING	INCREMENTAL
YEAR 1			
YEAR 2			
YEAR 3			
YEAR 4			
YEAR 5			
YEAR 6			

(8-31) *Finding the Terminal Cash Flow*

The *Terminal Cash Flow* is an after-tax cash flow from the termination and liquidation of a project at the end of its expected useful life

① Salvage value on new equipment + $
② Tax on sale of new equipment − $
③ Salvage value on old equipment − $
④ Working Capital + $

8-32   *Finding the Terminal Cash Flow*

To lend closure to the analysis, the firm must end up where it started, i.e. without the asset

8-33   *Finding the Terminal Cash Flow*

The terminal cash flow is equal to:
    After-Tax proceeds from sale of new asset
- After-Tax proceeds from sale of old asset
+ Change in net working capital

» If an asset is sold for a price different from its *book value*, there will be tax considerations
  - If sale price > Book Value, Tax > 0
  - If sale price < Book Value, Tax < 0

» Change in net working capital must be considered to reflect the reversion to the original status of any net working capital investment included in the initial investment (i.e., end where the firm started)

8-34   *Example*

- Continuing with the Torbert Company example, assume the new machine can be liquidated for $5,000 (after removal costs) at the end of its five-year useful life. The old machine would be obsolete and worth $0 at the same point in time. Torbert expects to recover its $1,500 net working capital investment at the termination of the project. Once again, the tax rate on both ordinary income and capital gains is 40%

To calculate the terminal cash flow, we must determine the taxes on the sale of the new machine

(Sale Price - Book Value) x Tax Rate

Example

8-35

Substituting the appropriate values into the terminal
cash flow calculation format, we find:

Proceeds from sale of new machine

-    Tax on sale of new machine

-    Proceeds from sale of old machine

+   Tax on sale of old machine

+   Change in net working capital   _____

=   Terminal Cash Flow   _____

Summarizing the Relevant Cash Flows

8-36

All three major cash flow components can be
summarized on a time line

Using the data from the Torbert Company examples:

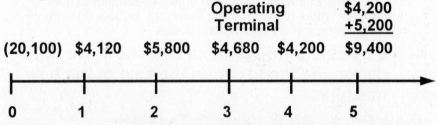

				Operating	$4,200
				Terminal	+5,200
(20,100)	$4,120	$5,800	$4,680	$4,200	$9,400

```
    ├────────┼────────┼────────┼────────┼────────┼──────────►

    0        1        2        3        4        5
```

NOTE: Since the asset is assumed to be sold at
the end of its useful life (Year 5), the incremental
operating cash inflow calculated for Year 6 is
irrelevant

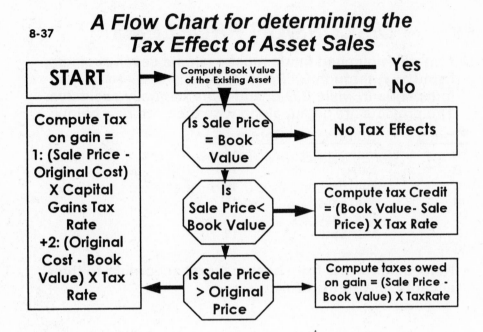

A Flow Chart for determining the Tax Effect of Asset Sales

8-37

8-38   **DISCUSSION PROBLEMS**

A firm with unlimited funds must evaluate seven projects, listed as A through G. Projects A, B, and G are independent, while C,D,E, and F are mutually exclusive. The projects are listed, along with their returns, below:

Project	Status	Return (%)
A	Ind.	11
B	Ind.	14
C	Mut. Excl.	10
D	Mut. Excl.	11
E	Mut. Excl.	13
F	Mut. Excl.	12
G	Ind.	15

• Rank the projects from best to worst according to their acceptability to the firm

8-39   *Answer*

Project	Status	Return (%)

8-40   ## *DISCUSSION PROBLEM*

- **Explain why a replacement project might still be acceptable to a firm even though the change in revenue resulting from the replacement is zero**

- **Answer:**

8-41   *DISCUSSION PROBLEM*

A machine was purchased two years ago for $100,000 and is being depreciated under the MACRS schedule using a five-year recovery period. What are the tax effects if the asset is sold for $150,000? (Assume a tax rate of 40% on both ordinary income and capital gains)

8-42   *Answer*

Compute the book value

Compute the gain on sale

Tax on sale:

recaptured depreciation makes up:

capital gains makes up:

9-1

Capital Budgeting Techniques: Certainty, Risk, and Some Refinements

- **Capital Budgeting Techniques**
- **Comparing NPV And IRR Techniques**
- **Approaches For Dealing With Risk**
- **Risk-Adjustment Techniques**
- **Capital Budgeting Refinements**

9-2   *Capital Budgeting Techniques*

- **Capital budgeting techniques are used to evaluate the acceptability of each project in order to make:**
  - **Accept/Reject Decisions**
  - **Ranking Decisions**

9-3
Example

(The data from this example will be used to illustrate each capital budgeting technique)

Discount Rate = 13%

	PROJECT	
	A	**B**
Initial Investment	$53,000	$50,000
Year	Operating Cash Inflows	
1	$25,000	$17,500
2	20,000	17,500
3	15,000	17,500
4	10,000	17,500

9-4
Payback Period

Payback Period is the amount of time it takes for a firm to recover its initial investment in a project as calculated from cash inflows

- Annuity Cash Inflows

$$\text{Payback Period} = \frac{\text{Initial Investment}}{\text{Amount of One Annual Cash Inflow}}$$

- For a non-annuity add up cumulative cash inflows until the initial investment has been fully recovered

9-5   *Example*

Project B is an annuity of $17,500

$$\frac{\text{Initial Investment}}{\text{Annuity Cash Inflow}} = \frac{\$50,000}{\$17,500} = \underline{\underline{}}$$

Project A is a mixed stream of cash inflows

<u>Year 1</u> + <u>Year 2</u> + <u>Part of Year 3</u>   = <u>Recovery of Initial Investment</u>

= $\underline{\underline{}}$

9-6   *Decision Criteria*

- **Accept if calculated payback period is less than maximum acceptable payback period**

- **If mutually exclusive, the preferred project is the one with the shortest acceptable payback period**

9-7 *Pros and Cons of Payback*

Pros

– Considers cash flows, not accounting profits
– Gives some implicit consideration to timing
– Gives some insight to risk exposure

Cons

– Cannot be expressed in terms of the wealth maximization goal
– Fails to consider explicitly the time value of money
– Fails to consider cash inflows after the payback period is reached

9-8 *Net Present Value*

- Net Present Value (NPV) is the amount of value added to (or subtracted from) a firm as the result of implementing a proposed project
- A sophisticated technique that considers the time value of money
- The discount rate is also often called:
  - Opportunity cost
  - Cost of capital
  - Required return

9-9   **NPV is calculated as:**

$$NPV = \sum_{i=1}^{n} \frac{CF_t}{(1 + k)^t} - II$$

= Present Value of Cash Inflows - Initial Investment

9-10   *Example*

Project A

Year	Cash Inflow	x	PVIF@13%	=	PV of Inflow
1	$ 25,000		.885		$22,125
2	20,000		.783		15,660
3	15,000		.693		10,395
4	10,000		.613		6,130
	PV of Inflows				$54,310
	Initial Investment				- 53,000
					= $ 1,310 = NPV$_A$

9-11   *Example*

Project B

($17,500) x (PVIFA$_{13\%,4}$) = 17,500 x (2.974) = $52,045 (PV of Inflows)
NPV$_B$ = $52,045 - $50,000 = <u>$2,045</u>

➡**Decision Criterion:**

Accept if NPV is greater than $0

NOTE: The higher the (positive) NPV, the more preferred is a given project

9-12   *Example*

Both project A (NPV = $1,310) and project B (NPV = $2,045) are acceptable, but B would be preferred over A in terms of ranking

- **NOTE: Choosing the proper discount rate is of utmost importance for validating the NPV methodology**

9-13   **Internal Rate of Return**

Internal Rate Of Return (IRR) is the actual rate of return earned by a project's discounted cash inflows, i.e., the discount rate makes the NPV equal $0

- **NOTE: IRR is the same idea as computing the yield-to-maturity of a bond**

9-14   **Mathematically, IRR is calculated by solving:**

$$\sum_{t=1}^{n} \frac{CF_t}{(1 + IRR)^t} = II$$

- **PV of Cash Inflows = Initial Investment**

A Trial-and-Error Approach must be used to calculate IRR by hand

9-15   ***Example***

For an annuity (Project B)
  Calculate payback period

$$\frac{\$50,000}{\$17,500} = \underline{\underline{}}$$

  Use PVIFA table to begin trial and error approach

9-16   ***Interpolate to find actual IRR***

9-17   *Example*

9-18   *Example*

9-19   **_Decision criterion:_**

Accept if IRR > cost of capital (discount rate)

NOTE: **The higher the IRR, the more preferred is a given project**

9-20   **_Example_**

9-21

Comparison of NPV and IRR Techniques

• **Basic Underlying Premise**

  –**NPV and IRR will always generate the same accept/reject decision for conventional projects at a given cost of capital**

  –**NPV and IRR, however, will sometimes rank projects differently due to differences in their underlying assumptions**

9-22

NPV Profiles

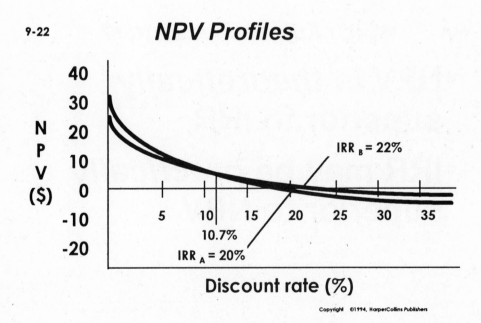

Copyright ©1994, HarperCollins Publishers

9-23   ## *Net Present Value Profiles*

- **By graphically depicting the relationship between particular discount rates and their resulting net present values for two or more projects, comparisons between the projects are enhanced**
- **At the point where the net present value profile lines cross for any two projects ("indifference point") the projects would be equivalent, i.e. they result in the same NPV for that particular discount rate**
- **Up to the indifference point one project will be superior to the other project, but after the indifference point the superiority reverses**
- **Note: NPV profiles do not always cross; when they don't, the NPV and IRR techniques will agree with respect to project ranking**

9-24   ## *Which Approach is Better?*

•NPV is *theoretically* superior to IRR

•IRR may be *practically* superior to NPV

Approaches for Dealing With Risk

9-25

• Risk and Cash Inflows

- –Few capital budgeting projects have the same level of risk as the firm
- –Risk refers to the variability of cash flows, typically *cash inflows*
- –Risk and cash flows are of most importance

9-26   *Example*

A firm is considering a project with an initial investment of $20,000. The life of the project is 12 years and the firm's cost of capital is 11%. For projects of this type, compute the breakeven cash inflow for the project

$$NPV = [CF \times (PVIFA_{11\%,12})] - II > 0$$

$$or \quad CF \times (PVIFA_{11\%,12}) > II$$

Thus CF =

9-27   *Sensitivity and Scenario Analysis*

An approach that attempts to capture the variability of cash inflows and NPV's

Sensitivity Analysis **uses a number of possible values for a given variable to assess its impact on return, as measured by NPV**

Scenario Analysis **is similar to sensitivity analysis but allows for simultaneous changes in a number of variables**

9-28   *Simulation*

- **Simulation is a statistically-based approach using probability distributions and random numbers to estimate risky outcomes**
- **The use of computers has made it possible to simulate virtually every inflow and outflow variable and determine the resulting NPV's**
- **After a thousand or so simulations the decision maker has a good idea of not only the expected value of the return on a project, but also the probability of achieving a given return**

International Risk Considerations

9-29

- **Two risks that can affect capital budgeting decisions**
  - **Exchange rate risk**
  - **Political risk**
- **Hedging instruments can be used to minimize exchange rate risk**
- **Subjectively account for political risk by adjusting cash flows for the probability of political interference**
- **Other considerations**
  - **Tax law differences**
  - **Transfer pricing**
  - **Strategic point of view**

9-30   *Risk Adjustment Techniques*

Certainty Equivalents (CE's) adjust cash inflows to determine the percentage of estimated inflows that investors would be satisfied to receive for certain in exchange for those that are possible each year

NPV when CE's are used is calculated as:

$$NPV = \sum_{t=1}^{n} = \frac{\alpha_t \times CF_t}{(1 + R_F)^t} - II$$

WHERE:

α_t = Certainty Equivalent factor in year t ($0 \leq \alpha_t \leq 1$)

CF_t = Relevant cash inflow in year t

R_F = Risk-free rate of return

Analysis of Bennett Company's Projects A and B Using Certainty Equivalents

9-31

Project A

Year (t)	Cash Inflows (1)	Certainty equivalents factors (2)	Certain Cash inflows [(1)X(2)] (3)	PVIF6%,t (4)	Present Value [(3)x(4)] (5)
1	$14,000	.90	$12,600	.943	$11,882
2	14,000	.90	12,600	.890	11,214
3	14,000	.80	11,200	.840	9,408
4	14,000	.70	9,800	.792	7,762
5	14,000	.60	8,400	.747	6,275

Present value of cash inflows $46,541
- Initial investment 42,000
= Net present value $ 4,541

Analysis of Bennett Company's Projects A and B Using Certainty Equivalents

9-32

Project B

Year (t)	Cash Inflows (6)	Certainty equivalents factors (7)	Certain Cash inflows [(6)X(7)] (8)	PVIF6%,t (9)	Present Value [(8)x(9)] (10)
1	$28,000	1.00	$28,000	.943	$26,404
2	12,000	.90	10,800	.890	9,612
3	10,000	.90	9,000	.840	7,560
4	10,000	.80	8,000	.792	6,336
5	10,000	.70	7,000	.747	5,229

Present value of cash inflows $55,141
- Initial investment 45,000
= Net present value $10,141

9-33   ***Risk-Adjustment Techniques***

Risk-Adjusted Discount Rates (RADR's) adjust for risk by changing the discount rate -- raising it for higher risk and lowering it for lower risk

RADR's are calculated as

$$NPV = \sum_{t=1}^{n} \frac{CF_t}{(1 + RADR)^t} - II$$

- **The use of RADRs is closely linked to the capital asset pricing model (CAPM)**

9-34   ***RADR and CAPM***

Recall that

   total risk = nondiversifiable risk + diversifiable risk

Beta is a measure of nondiversifiable risk and

$$k_j = R_F + [b_j \times (k_m - R_F)] \qquad (CAPM)$$

If we assume that real corporate assets are traded in efficient markets, CAPM can be modified as follows:

$$k_{Project\,j} = R_F + [b_{Project} \times (k_m - R_F)]$$

WHERE:

   $b_{Project}$ **is the relationship between the project's expected return and the market's expected return**

9-35

RADR and CAPM

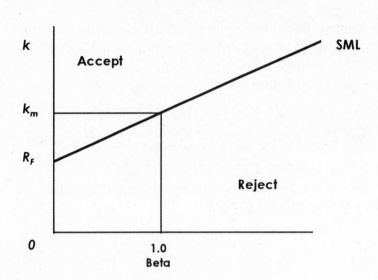

9-36

Applying RADRs

- **Since real corporate assets are not traded in an efficient market, total risk must be considered**

- **The coefficient of variation (CV) is used to measure total risk**

- **The firm must develop a market risk-return function depicting discount rates associated with various levels of project risk**

Applying RADR's

9-37

- **RADR is a function of the risk-free rate plus a risk premium, which is the amount by which a project's required discount rate exceeds the risk-free rate**

Analysis of Bennett Company's Projects A and B using Risk-Adjusted Discount Rates

9-38

Project A

Annual cash inflow	$14,000
X PVIFA $_{14\%,5\ yrs.}$	3.433
Present value of cash inflows	$48,062
- Initial investment	42,000
Net present value (NPV)	$ 6,062

Project B

Year (t)	Cash inflows (1)	PVIF11%,t (2)	Present Value [(1)x(2)] (3)
1	$28,000	.901	$25,228
2	12,000	.812	9,744
3	10,000	.731	7,310
4	10,000	.659	6,590
5	10,000	.593	5,930
	Present value of cash inflows		$54,802
	- Initial investment		45,000
	Net present value (NPV)		$ 9,802

9-39   *Portfolio Effects*

- **The value of the firm is generally *not* affected by diversification**

- **The market for real corporate assets is inefficient, therefore total risk is most relevant**

9-40   *CE Versus RADR in Practice*

- **CEs are theoretically preferred**

- **RADRs have mathematical problems but have operational appeal**

- **Firms often create risk classes for project proposals and assign a RADR to each risk class**

9-41 Bennett Company's Risk Classes and RADR's

Risk Class	Description	Risk-adjusted discount rate, RADR
I	*Below average risk:* Projects with low risk. Typically involve routine replacemet without renewal of existing activities.	8%
II	*Average risk:* Projects similar to those currently implemented. Typically involve replacement or renewal of existing activities.	10%
III	*Above-average risk:* Projects with higher than normal, but not excessive, risks. Typically involve expansion of existing or similar activities.	14%
IV	*Highest risk:* Projects with very high risk. Typically involve expansion into new or unfamiliar activities.	20%

9-42 Capital Budgeting Refinements

• **Comparing Projects With Unequal Lives**
  – The impact of differing lives must be considered
  – Annualized net present value (ANPV) approach
  STEPS:
   ❶ Calculate the NPV of each project

   ❷ Divide the NPV of each project by the PVIFA at the given cost of capital and life of the project to determine the annualized NPV (ANPV) for each project

   ❸ The project with the highest ANPV would be the most preferred

9-43

Example

The Spivey Corporation is considering two projects, J and T, whose relevant cash flows are given below. The projects are considered of equivalent risk and will thus be discounted at the same cost of capital, 13%

	PROJECT J	PROJECT T
Initial Investment	$35,000	$51,000
Year	Cash Inflows	
1	$14,000	$18,000
2	13,000	18,000
3	21,000	13,000
4	---	13,000
5	---	13,000

9-44

Example

Step 1

$NPV_J =$

$NPV_T =$

9-45   *Example*

Step 2

$ANPV_J =$

$ANPV_T =$

Step 3

9-46   *Capital Rationing*

- **Capital Rationing is a financial condition occurring when there are more acceptable projects than funds available to finance them**
  - **The objective of capital rationing is to find the projects that provide the highest overall NPV without exceeding the amount of funds budgeted for capital projects**
  - **There are two popular approaches used in capital rationing**
    - » **Internal rate of return approach**
    - » **The net present value approach**

9-47   *Example*

The De Moura Company has identified five projects
that are competing for funding from its $200,000
fixed capital budget. The firm has a cost of capital
of 12%. The data concerning the projects are
summarized below:

Project	Initial Investment	IRR	PV of Inflows @ 12%
A	$100,000	16%	$112,500
B	75,000	14%	84,000
C	125,000	11%	120,000
D	90,000	17%	105,000
E	110,000	15%	124,500

9-48   **The IRR Approach**

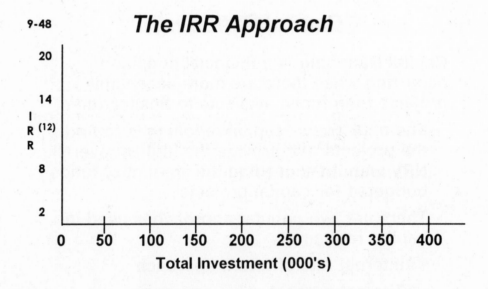

9-49
The NPV Approach

Project   IRR   NPV of Inflows

9-50
DISCUSSION PROBLEMS

Stockton Enterprises is considering expanding its oil drilling operations. Under consideration is a new platform rig requiring an initial investment of $12,000,000. With the new rig net cash inflows are expected to increase by $2,750,000 per year over the 15-year useful life of the rig. Stockton requires a 25% return (after tax) on all investments of the type due to the riskiness of the operations. Should Stockton purchase the new rig?

Determine NPV of Project

NPV =

9-51   ## DISCUSSION PROBLEMS

Domanski Manufacturing is considering a project which
is expected to generate new cash inflows of $1,750,000
over the next 8 years. The initial investment is
$7,500,000. If Domanski's management wishes to
know the IRR for the projects, at what rate (from the
PVIFA table) should the trial-and-error process begin?

9-52   ## DISCUSSION PROBLEMS

The Gunnison Office Supply Company has computed the
IRR of a project to be exactly 19%. If the project has a
five-year life and its cash inflows are in annuity form,
what is the value of one cash inflow given an initial
investment of $20,000?

The Cost of Capital

10-1

- **An Overview Of The Cost Of Capital**
- **The Cost Of Long-Term Debt**
- **The Cost Of Preferred Stock**
- **The Cost Of Common Stock**
- **The Weighted Average Cost Of Capital (WACC)**
- **The Marginal Cost And Investment Decisions**

An Overview Of The Cost Of Capital

10-2

- **The cost of capital has two important definitions**
  - The rate of return a firm must earn on its projects or investments to maintain the market value of its stock, assuming constant risk
  - The rate of return required by the market suppliers of capital to attract their funds to the firm

10-3   *Basic Assumptions*

•Business Risk

•Financial Risk

•After-Tax Costs

10-4   *Risk of Financing Costs*

- The general relationship between risk and financing costs can be explained by the following equation:

$$k_l = R_F + b_p + f_p$$

WHERE:

k_l = specific cost of a given source of long-term financing, 1

R_F = risk-free cost of a given type of financing, 1

b_p = business risk premium

f_p = financial risk premium

- NOTE: This is simply another version of the nominal rate of interest equation $(k_l = R_F + RP_l)$

10-5   *Risk of Financing Costs*

• The equation can be evaluated in two ways:

–Times-Series Comparisons
–Cross-Sectional Comparisons

10-6   *The Basic Concept*

- **Cost of capital is measured at a given point in time**
- **Cost of capital reflects the cost of funds over the long run**
- **Cost of capital reflects the interrelatedness of financing activities**
- **Cost of capital assumes a deliberate financing mix called a *target capital structure***
- **Given the target capital structure, the firm's overall cost of capital - often measured as the "weighted average cost of capital" - is of greatest importance**

Example

10-7

- **A firm that has a target capital structure of 40% debt and 60% equity should consider the long run overall cost of capital when making capital budgeting decisions. If, for example, debt financing is available at a cost of 8% (after tax) and equity financing is available at a cost of 15%, the weighted average long-term cost of capital is [(.40 x 8%) + (.60 x 15%)] = 12.2%, reflecting the interrelatedness of financing decisions. Decisions made with the weighted average cost of capital in mind generally are in the best interests of the firm and its shareholders.**

The Cost of Specific Sources of Capital

10-8

- **There are four basic sources of long-term funds**
  - **Long-term debt**
  - **Preferred stock**
  - **Common stock**
  - **Retained earnings**

- **The specific cost of each source of financing is the after-tax cost of obtaining the financing today**
- **The techniques used to determine specific costs of capital generate rough approximations due to their numerous assumptions and underlying forecasts**

The Cost of Long-Term Debt (Bonds)

10-9

- **Preliminary Assumptions:**
  - Funds are raised through the issuance and sale of bonds
  - The bonds pay annual interest
- **Net Proceeds**
  - » *Net Proceeds* are the funds the firm actually receives from the sale of a security
  - » *Flotation Costs* are the total costs incurred by the firm in issuing and selling a security
  - » Net proceeds = selling price of the security - flotation costs

Before-Tax Cost of Debt

10-10

- **The Before-Tax Cost of Debt must be obtained first, by one of three possible methods**
  - ❶ Using cost quotations
    - » If net proceeds are equal to the bond's par value, the before-tax cost is equal to the bond's coupon interest rate
    - » The yield-to-maturity of similar-risk bonds can also be used as an estimate of before-tax cost
  - ❷ Calculating the cost, using the cost-to-maturity, which is the internal rate of return on the bond's cash flows from the issuers point of view
  - ❸ Approximating the cost using the approximation formula

10-11

Example

**A firm sells some 25-year bonds at par of $1,000.
Flotation costs are 1 1/2% of par. The coupon interest
rate is 12%. Find the before-tax cost of debt (k_d). [net
proceeds = $1,000-[.015 x ($1,000) = $985]**

Relevant Cash Flows   NPV @12% = -$15 (try it yourself!)

End of Year(s)	Cash Flow
0	$ 985
1-25	$ (120)
25	$(1,000)

10-12

Approximating the cost with approximation formula:

$$k_d = \frac{I + \dfrac{\$1,000 - N_d}{n}}{(N_d + 1,000) / 2}$$

WHERE:

I   =   **Annual interest payment (in dollars)**

N_d =   **Net proceeds per bond**

n   =   **Number of years to maturity**

10-13   *Example*

Using data from previous example

10-14   *After-Tax Cost of Debt*

The after-tax cost of debt is calculated as:

$$k_i = k_d \times (1-T)$$

WHERE:

T = Tax rate of the firm

10-15   *Example*

Using the 12.2% before-tax cost of debt from the previous example's cost-to-maturity approach and a tax rate of 40%, the after-tax cost of debt is

$k_i =$

10-16   *The Cost of Preferred Stock*

- **Preferred Stock Dividends**
  - Preferred stockholders receive a stated dividend prior to the distribution of earnings to common stockholders
- **Preferred stock has an implied infinite life**
- **Preferred stock dividends are usually a stated dollar amount**
- **Alternatively, preferred stock dividends may be stated as an annual percentage rate, e.g., 7%**

Calculating the Cost of Preferred Stock

10-17

Calculating the cost of preferred stock is straightforward:

$$k_p = \frac{D_p}{N_p}$$

WHERE:

k_p = Cost of preferred stock

D_p = Annual dollar dividend per share

N_p = Net proceeds per share

10-18

Example

An issue of preferred stock was sold for $78 per share. The stock will pay $8 per year in dividends. Flotation costs of $3 per share were incurred by the firm. Find k_p

k_p =

10-19   *The Cost of Common Stock*

• There are two forms of common stock financing

–Retained earnings

–New issues of common stock

10-20   *Finding the Cost of Common Stock Equity*

- The Cost Of Common Equity (k_s) is the rate at which investors discount expected dividends to determine the share value of the firm

- Two techniques for measuring the cost of common stock equity capital are available

10-21

Constant Growth Valuation (Gordon) Model

$$P_o = \frac{D_1}{k_s - g}$$ **Can Be Rewritten As**

$$k_s = \frac{D_1}{P_o} + g$$ **(Dividend Yield + Growth Rate)**

10-22

Example

A firm's stock is currently selling for $22 per share, it expects to pay a dividend of $1.76 per share next year, and dividends have been growing at a compound annual rate of 5%. Find k_s?

$$k_s = \frac{\$1.76}{\$22} + .05$$

$$k_s = 13\%$$

10-23
Capital Asset Pricing Model (CAPM)

$$k_s = R_F + [b \times (k_m - R_F)]$$

10-24
Example

If a firm's Beta is 1.25, the risk-free rate is 6%, and the market return is 11.5%, find k_s.

$$k_s =$$

10-25 *Comparing the Gordon and CAPM Techniques*

- **CAPM directly incorporates risk with the use of Beta to get a required return**
- **Gordon Model uses market price as a reflection of risk-return preferences of investors**
- **The Gordon Model is generally preferred because**
  - Better data is available (i.e., stock prices)
  - Can adjust readily for flotation costs to find the cost of new issues of common stock

10-26 *The Cost of Retained Earnings*

- **The Cost of Retained Earnings is essentially the same as the cost of common stock equity**
  - Retained earnings increase the stockholders' equity in the same way as a new issue of common stock
  - Stockholders accept the firm's retention of earnings as long as they expect those earnings to return to them a rate equal to their required return on the reinvested funds
- **Thus, the cost of retained earnings (k_r) is equal to k_s, and either the Gordon Model or CAPM can be used to determine it**

10-27 *The Cost of New Issues of Common Stock*

Must consider:
Underpricing

Flotation Costs

$N_n = P_o$ - *Underpricing - Flotation Costs*

10-28 *Cost of a new stock issue (k_n) is calculated as:*

$$k_n = \frac{D_1}{N_n} + g$$

- NOTE: Since N_n is always less than P_o, k_n is always greater than k_r

10-29

Example

The firm in the previous example will have to underprice the new shares by $1.00 each from their current price of $22, plus incur a $2.00 per share flotation cost in order to sell them. Find k_n

N_n = $22 - $1 -$2 = $19

D_1 = $1.76

g = 5%

k_n =

10-30

Calculating the WACC

- **The weighted average cost of capital (WACC) is computed with the use of the corporation's existing capital structure**
  - Determine the percentage composition of each source of capital in the capital structure (The "Weight")
  - Multiply the specific cost of each source of capital by its weight
  - Sum the products and you have the WACC

10-31   *Weighing schemes*

- **Book Value Weights**
- **Market Value Weights**
- **Historic Weights**
- **Target Weights**

10-32   *WACC (k_a) is calculated as:*

$$k_a = (w_i \times k_i) + (w_p \times k_p) + (w_s \times k_r \text{ or } k_n)$$

WHERE:

w_i = **Proportion of L-T debt in the capital structure**

w_p = **Proportion of preferred stock in the capital structure**

w_s = **Proportion of common equity in the capital structure**

Note: $w_i + w_p + w_s = 1.0$

10-33   *Example*

The Reyes Company seeks a target capital structure of
40% long-term debt, 20% preferred stock, and 40%
common stock equity. Assuming that Reyes can obtain
long-term financing at the after tax costs of 7.32% for
debt, 10.67% for preferred stock, and 13% for common
stock equity, find k_a

k_a =

If Reyes needs to sell new common stock to maintain the
target capital structure, substitute k_n for k_s (k_n = 14.26%)

k_a =

10-34   *The Marginal Cost and
Investment Decisions*

• A firm's financing costs and
investment returns will be affected
by the volume of financing/
investment undertaken.

– Investors' perceptions of rising business risk

– Investors' perceptions of rising financial risk

– Size of the investment(s)

– ^Financing Levels; ^ Uncertainty; ^Risk;
^ Required Returns

The Marginal Cost and Investment Decision

10-35

- **The marginal cost of capital is the cost of the next dollar of financing obtained**
- **Investment decisions should be based upon the criterion that a project's expected return must be greater than the weighted marginal cost of capital (WMCC) for the firm**

The Weighted Marginal Cost Of Capital (WMCC)

10-36

The weighted average cost of capital will rise whenever there is a rise in the cost of any one of the capital sources

The level of total financing at which the cost of one of the capital sources rises is called a *breaking point* (BP_j)

$$BP_j = \frac{Af_j}{wj}$$

WHERE:

BP_j = Breaking point for financing source *j*

AF_j = Amount of funds available from financing source *j* at a given cost

w_j = Capital structure weight for financing source *j*

10-37

Example

The Duchess Corporation has $300,000 of retained earnings available at a cost (k_r) of 13%. If it exhausts retained earnings, it must use new common stock at a cost (k_n) of 14%. Additionally, the firm expects it can raise up to $400,000 of long-term debt at a cost (k_i) of 5.6%; any further use of debt will be at a cost of 8.4%. The firm can issue an unlimited number of shares of preferred stock at a cost (k_p) of 10.6%. The target capital structure is 40% L-T debt, 50% common equity, and 10% preferred stock.

10-38

Example

Computing the breaking points is straightforward

$$BP_{\text{Common Equity}} =$$

$$BP_{\text{L-T Debt}} =$$

Weighted Average Cost of Capital for Ranges of Total New Financing for Duchess Corporation

10-39

Range of Total New Financing	Source of Capital (1)	Weight (2)	Cost (3)	Weighted Cost [(2) x (3)] (4)
$0 to $600,000	Debt	.40	5.6%	2.2%
	Preferred	.10	10.6	1.1
	Common	.50	13.0	6.5
	Weighted average cost of capital			9.8%
$600,000 to $1,000,000	Debt	.40	5.6%	2.2%
	Preferred	.10	10.6	1.1
	Common	.50	14.0	7.0
	Weighted average cost of capital			10.3%
$1,000,000 and above	Debt	.40	8.4%	3.4%
	Preferred	.10	10.6	1.1
	Common	.50	14.0	7.0
	Weighted average cost of capital			11.5%

10-40

Graph The WMCC

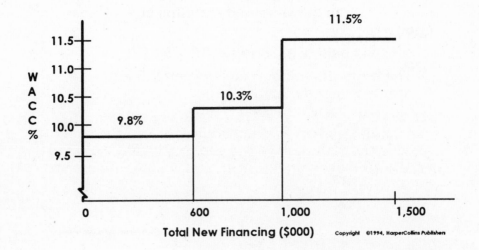

The Investment Opportunities Schedule (IOS)

10-41

- A firm's IOS is simply a list of the firm's investment opportunities ranked (from best to worst) by the internal rates of return (IRR) of the investments
- A firm will generally choose to invest in those opportunities with the highest returns first and continue to finance investments (assuming capital is available) up to the point at which the marginal return on its investments equals its weighted marginal cost of capital

Making Financing/Investing Decisions

10-42

- The firm should accept all projects for which the IRR is greater than the weighted marginal cost of new financing
  - NPV is positive as long as IRR > k_a
  - The larger the difference between IRR and k_a, the greater the resulting NPV
- By plotting the firm's WMCC Schedule and its investment opportunity schedule (IOS) on the same set of axes, it is possible to see graphically both the firm's optimal capital budget, and which projects will be financed

10-43 *IOS and WMCC Schedules*

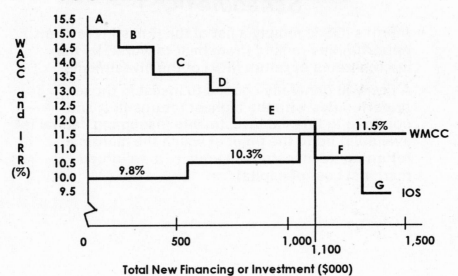

10-44   *DISCUSSION PROBLEMS*

A firm expects to have $400,000 in retained earnings available in the next year. Given the following target capital structure, at what level of total new financing will retained earnings be exhausted?

Financing Source	Target Proportion
L-T Debt	40%
Preferred Stock	20
Common Stock Equity	40
Total	100%

10-45   *DISCUSSION PROBLEMS*

- **The Spivey Corporation has just sold, without incurring floatation costs, some 20-year bonds with a coupon interest rate of 13% at par. If the corporation is in the 40% tax bracket, what is the after-tax cost of debt?**

10-46   *DISCUSSION PROBLEMS*

If Spivey is able to sell preferred stock at 15% and raise common equity at 16.5%, what is the corporation's weighted average cost of capital when its target capital structure is 30% debt, 55% common stock equity, and 15% preferred stock?

$K_a =$

10-47   *DISCUSSION PROBLEMS*

The Morris Company is attempting to determine its cost of capital in order to evaluate several proposed capital projects and set its capital budget for next year. The following information has been made available:

- Target capital structure is 40% debt, 60% common stock equity
- $10 million can be borrowed at a pre-tax cost of 11%
- Additional debt will cost 14% (pre-tax) but is unlimited
- $7,500,000 of retained earnings will be generated next year
- Additional common equity will be raised through issuing new common stock (no limit foreseen)
- Morris stock currently sells for $12.00 per share
- Last year's dividend was $1.20
- Dividends are expected to grow 4% annually
- New common stock will be sold for $11.00 per share and flotation costs will be $1.00 per share
- Morris is in the 40% tax bracket

10-48   *Cost of Capital:*

What is Morris' cost of capital?

Determine cost of capital for each financing source:

Cost of Debt:
    First $10,000,000   =
    Additional Debt   =

Cost of Common stock Equity:
    Retained Earnings   =

    New Common Stock =

Cost of Capital:

10-49

Determine break points and associated WACCs

$$BP_{Common\ Equity} =$$

$$BP_{LT\ Debt} =$$

Weighted Average Cost of Capital

Range	WACC
$0 to $12,500,000	
$12,500,000 to $25,000,000	
$25,000,000 and above	

Cost of Capital:

10-50

11-1   *Leverage and Capital Structure*

- **Leverage**
- **The Firm's Capital Structure**
- **The EBIT-EPS Approach To Capital Structure**
- **Choosing The Optimal Capital Structure**

11-2   *Leverage*

- **Leverage is the use of Fixed-Cost Assets or Funds to magnify returns to the firm's owners**
- **There is a direct relationship between leverage and risk/return**

11-3   *Leverage*

There are three types of leverage

- **Operating Leverage**
- **Financial Leverage**
- **Total Leverage**

General Income Statement Format and Types of Leverage

11-4

Operating Leverage	Sales revenue Less: Cost of goods sold Gross profits Less: Operating expenses Earnings before interest and taxes (EBIT)
Financial Leverage	Less: Intersest Net profit before taxes Less: Taxes Net profit after taxes Less: Preferred stock dividends Earnings available for common stockholders Earnings per share (EPS)

Total Leverage

11-5

Breakeven Analysis

- The Operating Breakeven Point
- Fixed Operating Costs
- Variable Operating Costs
- The Algebraic Approach uses the following variables

P = Sale price per unit

Q = Sales quantity in units

FC = Fixed operating cost per period

VC = Variable operating cost per unit

$$EBIT = (P \times Q) - FC - (VC \times Q)$$
$$= Q \times (P - VC) - FC$$
$$\$0 = Q \times (P - VC) - FC$$
$$Q = \frac{FC}{P-VC}$$

11-6

Example

A firm has fixed operating costs of $2,500, a $10 sale price per unit, and a $5 per unit variable operating cost. Compute its operating breakeven point

$$Q =$$

The operating breakeven point can also be determined by the graphic approach

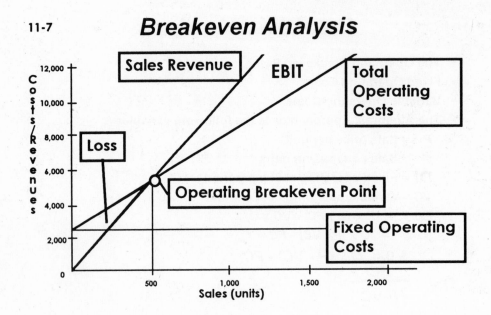

11-7 *Breakeven Analysis*

Breakeven Analysis

11-8

- **Changing costs and the operating breakeven point**
    - An increase in either fixed cost or variable cost will raise the breakeven point and vice versa
    - An increase in sales price will lower the break even point and vice versa

11-9   *Operating Leverage*

Operating leverage works in both ways, i.e. if a firm has fixed operating costs, an increase in sales will result in a more-than-proportional increase in EBIT, and a decrease in sales will result in a more-than-proportional decrease in EBIT

11-10   Example

Assume a firm with: FC = $2,500; P = $10; VC = $5, and a current Q of 1,000 units

11-11 *Measuring the Degree of Operating Leverage (DOL)*

- DOL is a numeric measure of the firm's operating leverage
- DOL is calculated as:

$$DOL = \frac{\% \text{ Change in EBIT}}{\% \text{ Change in Sales}}$$

or

DOL at base sales level Q

$$= \frac{Q \times (P - VC)}{Q \times (P - VC) - FC}$$

11-12 *Example*

Using data from the previous example

DOL @ 1,000 units =

11-13

Fixed Costs And Operating Leverage

- **Changes in fixed operating costs affect operating leverage significantly**

- **If, for example, a firm can shift some of its variable costs to fixed costs, it will increase the DOL and magnify the relationship between sales and EBIT even further**

11-14

Example

- **From the previous example assume that the following shift occurs:**

  ## VC reduced to $4.50/unit
  ## FC increased to $3,000

11-15

Operating leverage and Increased Fixed Costs

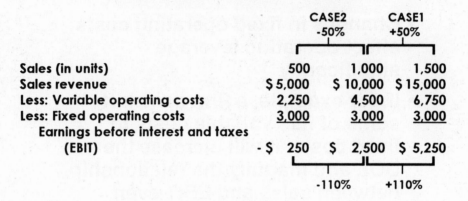

	CASE2 -50%		CASE1 +50%
Sales (in units)	500	1,000	1,500
Sales revenue	$ 5,000	$ 10,000	$ 15,000
Less: Variable operating costs	2,250	4,500	6,750
Less: Fixed operating costs	3,000	3,000	3,000
Earnings before interest and taxes (EBIT)	- $ 250	$ 2,500	$ 5,250
	-110%		+110%

11-16

Example

DOL @ 1,000 units =

11-17   *Financial Leverage*

- Financial leverage also works both ways, i.e. an increase in the firm's EBIT will result in a more-than-proportional increase in the firm's EPS, and vice versa, as long as the firm is using fixed financing costs
  - There are two fixed financial costs common to firms
    - » Interest on debt
    - » Preferred stock dividends
  - Fixed financial costs must be paid regardless of how much EBIT there is available to pay them

11-18   *Example*

A firm expects its EBIT to be $10,000 next year. It pays $2,000 per year in interest expenses and $2,400 in annual preferred stock dividends. There are currently 1,000 shares of common stock outstanding
To analyze the effect of a 40% increase and a 40% decrease in EBIT on the firm's EPS see text Table 11.6 on page 447

Measuring the Degree of Financial Leverage (DFL)

11-19

DFL is a numerical measure of the firm's financial leverage

DFL is calculated as:

$$DFL = \frac{\%\ Change\ in\ EPS}{\%\ Change\ in\ EBIT}$$

or

DFL @ base level of EBIT = $\dfrac{EBIT}{EBIT - I - (PD \times 1/(1-T))}$

WHERE:

I	=	Annual interest expense
PD	=	Preferred stock dividend
T	=	Tax rate

Example

11-20

Using data from previous example

DFL @ $10,000 EBIT =

11-21   *Total Leverage: The Combined Effect*

- **Total Leverage combines the effect of using both fixed operating and fixed financial costs to magnify the impact of changes in sales on the firm's EPS**

11-22   *Example*

- **Given a firm with the following data:**
- Price/unit   = $5
- Variable cost/unit   = $2
- Fixed operating costs   = $10,000
- Interest expense   = $20,000
- Preferred stock dividends   = $12,000
- Marginal tax rate   = 40%
- Common stock shares outstanding = 5,000
- Expected sales   = 20,000 units
- Potential sales   = 30,000 units

11-23   *The Total Leverage Effect*

Sales (in units)
Sales revenue
Less: Variable operating costs
Less: Fixed operating costs
    Earnings before interest
      and taxes (EBIT)

Less: Interest

Net profits before taxes
Less: Taxes (T = .40)
Net profits after taxes
Less: Preferred stock dividends
Earnings available for common

Earnings per share (EPS) =

11-24   *Measuring The Degree Of Total Leverage (DTL)*

- **DTL is a numeric measure of the firm's total leverage**
  DTL is calculated as:

$$DTL = \frac{\% \text{ Change in EPS}}{\% \text{ Change in Sales}}$$

    or

DTL @ base sales level Q

$$= \frac{Q \times (P - VC)}{Q \times (P-VC) - FC - I - (PD \times 1/(1-T))}$$

11-25

Example

Using data from previous example

DTL @ 20,000 units =

11-26

The Relationship of Operating, Financial, and Total Leverage

- **Note that the numerator of the DOL percentage change formula (EBIT) is the same as the denominator of the DFL percentage change formula (EBIT)**
  - Thus if you multiply the two formulas together, the EBITs cancel out
  - The remainder of the percentage change formula for the DTL

Thus, the following relationship exists:

DOL x DFL = DTL

11-27   *The Firm's Capital Structure*

- **Capital structure is a complex area of financial decision making due to the relationship between the firm's financing sources, the firm's risk/return profile, and the firm's value**

11-28   *Types of Capital*

- **Capital is a term referring to the long-term funds of the firm**
- **On the firm's balance sheet, all items on the right- hand side except current liabilities are capital**
- **There are two major types of capital**
  - **Debt Capital**
  - **Equity Capital**

11-29 External Assessment of Capital Structure

- Debt Ratios can be used to measure the firm's degree of financial leverage
  - Measurements of indebtedness
  - Measurements of ability to service debt
- The more risk a firm is willing to take, the greater will be its financial leverage
  - A firm should theoretically maintain a level of financial leverage consistent with the capital structure that maximizes shareholder wealth
  - There are significant differences in typical degrees of financial leverage between industries

11-30 Capital Structure of Non-U.S. Firms

- Non-U.S. companies tend to have much higher leverage ratios than do American companies
- Few countries have such developed capital markets as exist in the U.S. leaving those countries' banks as the major provider of (leveraged) funds
- Many foreign countries allow their banks to make equity investments in nonfinancial corporations - a practice currently prohibited for U.S. banks
- Share ownership in foreign corporations is rarely as broad -based as is ownership in U.S. companies

11-31 *Capital Structure of Non-U.S. Firms*

• Capital structure patterns among industries tend to be quite similar around the world

11-32   *Capital Structure Theory*

- How a chosen financing mix affects the firm's value has been a topic of considerable study
- Modigliani and Miller (hereafter "M & M") demonstrated algebraically that, assuming perfect markets, capital structure has no effect on the firm's value
- Subsequent research suggests the existence of an optimal capital structure based upon the balancing of the benefits and costs of debt financing
- The major benefit of debt financing is the tax deduct ibility of interest payments, making more earnings available for investors

11-33
The major costs of debt financing include:

- **The probability of bankruptcy due to an inability to meet obligations depends on:**
  - **–Business Risk**
  - **–Financial Risk**
- **Agency Costs Imposed by Lenders**
- **Asymmetric Information**

11-34
Asymetric Information

- If a firm's managers feel that the firm's stock is undervalued and there is an available investment that they feel will increase the value of the firm, the managers will use debt financing to fund it
- If a firm's managers feel that the firm's stock is overvalued, however, they will use a stock issue to finance the investment
- Management action (debt vs. new stock financing) is seen as a signal by investors in the marketplace
  - debt is generally seen as a positive signal
  - equity is generally seen as a negative signal

11-35   *The Optimal Capital Structure*

- The value of the firm is maximized when the cost of capital is minimized
- Assuming the zero growth valuation model, the value of the firm is calculated as:

$$V = \frac{EBIT \times (1-T)}{k_a}$$

WHERE:

V = Value of the firm

$EBIT \times (1-T)$ = After-tax operating earnings available to the debt and equity holders

k_a = Weighted average cost of capital. If EBIT is constant, value is maximized when the weighted average cost of capital is minimized

11-36   *Cost Functions*

- k_i = After-tax cost of debt
- k_s = Cost of equity
- k_a = Weighted average cost of capital

- The cost function graphs illustrate the behavior of the costs of debt and equity as their use increases by the firm. Their combined effect on the weighted average cost of capital is also shown.

A Graphic View of the Optimal Capital Structure

11-37

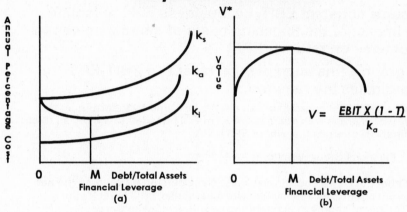

The EBIT-EPS Approach to Capital Structure

11-38

- The *EBIT-EPS Approach* is a method of selecting the firm's capital structure by determining the combination of funding sources that maximizes earnings per share (EPS) over the firm's expected range of earnings before interest and taxes (EBIT)

Presenting A Financial Plan Graphically

11-39

- **Assume constant EBIT, i.e. business risk, to isolate the impact of the financing costs of alternative capital structures on returns (EPS)**
- **To graph a financing plan, at least two EBIT-EPS coordinates are required**
  - One EBIT-EPS coordinate can always be found by determining the *financial breakeven point*, the level of EBIT needed to satisfy all fixed financial charges (i.e. where EPS = $0)

    $$\text{Financial Breakeven Point} = I + \frac{PD}{1-T}$$

  - Other EBIT-EPS coordinates must be calculated by dividing the net profit after taxes associated with a particular EBIT level by the number of shares of outstanding common stock in the capital structure

Each capital structure is superior for a particular range of EBIT

11-40

From		To	Optimal Capital Structure
$ 0	-	$50,000 EBIT	0% Debt
$50,000	-	$95,500 EBIT	30% Debt
>$95,500		EBIT	60% Debt

Also, the higher the financial breakeven point and the steeper the slope of the capital structure line, the greater the risk!

Finding EBIT-EPS Indifference Points Algebraically

11-41

- An algebraic method of solving for the indifference points between capital structure alternatives is also available for determining optimal capital structures:

- The formula for determining EPS for any capital structure is:

$$EPS = \frac{(1-T) \times (EBIT - I) - PD}{\text{No. of Shares of Common Stock Outstanding}}.$$

- By setting the equations for two capital structures equal to each other, you can solve for the level of EBIT at which you would be indifferent between the two structures, i.e. where EPS is the same

11-42

Example

Comparing the Cooke Company's 30% and 60% capital structures we get:

$$\frac{(1-.40) \times (EBIT - \$15.00) - \$0}{17.50} = \frac{(1-.40) \times (EBIT - \$49.50) - \$0}{10.00}$$

$$\frac{.60\ EBIT - \$9.00}{17.50} = \frac{.60\ EBIT - \$29.70}{10.00}$$

$$6\ EBIT - \$90.00 = 10.5\ EBIT - \$519.75$$

$$\$429.75 = 4.5\ EBIT$$

$$\underline{\$95.5 = EBIT}$$

Thus, at an EBIT level of $95.5 we are indifferent between the two structures. If EBIT is expected to be less than $95.5, we would choose the 30% debt structure. If EBIT is expected to be greater than $95.5, we would choose the 60% debt structure

11-43 *Considering Risk in EBIT-EPS Analysis*

- **Two points are important to understand:**
  - The higher the financial breakeven point, the greater the financial risk of the capital structure
  - The steeper the slope of the capital structure line, the greater the financial risk

- **Performing ratio analysis (times-interest-earned ratio) will substantiate these points**

11-44 *Example*

- **Given the data for the Cooke Company in Figure 11.6, the Times Interest Earned (TIE) ratios for the three capital structures are:**

STRUCTURE	EBIT/INTEREST	TIE
0% Debt	$100,000/0	∞
30% Debt	$100,000/$15,000	6.67
60% Debt	$100,000/$49,500	2.02

Since lower values of TIE reflect higher financial risk, it is obvious that higher levels of debt increase risk

11-45 *Basic Shortcomings of EBIT-EPS Analysis*

- **Since the objective is to maximize the EPS rather than shareholder wealth, the technique ignores risk**

- **Since risk premiums increase with increased financial leverage, the maximization of EPS does not assure owners' wealth maximization**

11-46 *Choosing the Optimal Capital Structure*

- **Return and risk must be integrated to determine the value of the firm under each alternative capital structure**
  - **The risk of each structure must be associated with the required rate of return for that structure**
  - **The use of CAPM is the preferred approach, but requires an estimate of Beta for each capital structure**
  - **Another approach is to link the required return directly to the capital structure through market observation/analysis, but requires the use of a statistic such as the coefficient of variation of EPS**
  - **Regardless of approach, required returns are expected to increase with increasing financial risk**

11-47

Example

Estimating Value

Assuming all earnings are paid out as dividends, the zero-growth valuation model can be used

$$P_o = \frac{EPS}{k_s}$$

By comparing the estimated share value under each capital structure alternative, we can determine which structure maximizes shareholder wealth

Thus, the 30% debt capital structure is optimal

Note that the capital structure that maximizes EPS (50% debt) is not the one that maximizes share value

11-48

Some Other Important Considerations

Business Risk
   Revenue stability
   Cash flow
Agency Costs
   Contractual obligations
   Management preferences
   Control
Asymmetric Information
   External risk assessment
   Timing

11-49   ## *DISCUSSION PROBLEMS*

- A company has current sales of $400,000; an EPS of $2.00 per share; a DOL of 1.3 and a DFL of 2.0. If the firm's sales are expected to increase by 10% next year, what will its EPS be?

- Compute DTL

    DTL =

- Compute EPS % Change

- Compute EPS

11-50   ## *DISCUSSION PROBLEM*

- Morris Manufacturing must raise $250 million to finance its proposed capital projects for next year. The finance committee is considering two possible financing plans. Plan A is to issue $250 million in 10% bonds. Plan B is to issue $100 million in 10% bonds and 10 million shares of common stock at $15 (net) per share. The current capital structure is 60% equity, including 35 million shares of common stock outstanding, and 40% debt, upon which the company pays $25 million per year in interest. If the company is in the 40% tax bracket, find the EBIT-EPS indifference point between the two financing plans

What we know without new financing of any kind:

$I =$; No. of Common Shares Outstanding =

New financing will add:

Plan A:

Plan B:

DISCUSSION PROBLEM

11-51

Thus:

EPS (Plan A)   =   EPS (Plan B)

DISCUSSION PROBLEM

11-52

Prove that $102.5 million is the indifference point

	Plan A	Plan B
EBIT		
- Interest		
= EBT		
Taxes @ 40%		
= Net Profit After Tax		
Shares Outstanding		
EPS =		

12-1

Long-Term Debt and Investment Banking

- **Characteristics of Long-Term Debt Financing**
- **Term Loans**
- **Corporate Bonds**
- **Investment Banking**

12-2

Characteristics of Long-Term Debt Financing

- **Long-term debt financing is financing with an initial maturity of more than one year (typically 5 to 20 years)**
- **Long-term debt financing may be raised either through:**
  - **Term Loans**
  - **Bonds**

Characteristics of Long-Term Debt Financing

12-3

- **Recall that long-term debt:**
  - Generally has a lower after-tax cost than equity financing for a particular firm
  - Provides financial leverage
  - Adds risk of bankruptcy and agency costs to the firm
- ***Investment Bankers* are institutions that assist in the private placement of debt issues, and play a major role in public offerings**

12-4   *Standard Debt Provisions*

- **The borrowing firm must:**
  - Maintain satisfactory accounting records
  - Supply audited financial statements
  - Pay taxes and other liabilities when due
  - Maintain all facilities in good working order

12-5   *Restrictive Debt Provisions*

- Maintaining a minimum level of net working capital to ensure liquidity
- Being prohibited from selling accounts receivable to avoid a long-run cash shortage
- Being prohibited from liquidating, acquiring, or encumbering any fixed assets since these actions could damage the borrower's ability to repay its debt
- Being prohibited from entering into any consolidation, merger, or other combination that could change the borrower's business and financial risk
- Having to spend the borrowed funds on a proven financial need
- Being required to maintain certain "key employees", without whom the borrower's future would be uncertain
- Having to subordinate any further debt to the original loan

12-6   *Restrictive Debt Provisions*

- **If the borrower violates any standard or restrictive provision, the lender may require immediate repayment of the loan**
- **Restrictive covenants address the agency problem created by the relationship between owners and creditors**

12-7   *Cost of Long-Term Debt*

•Is affected by:
- –Loan Maturity
- –Loan Size
- –Borrower Risk
- –Basic Cost Of Money

12-8   *Term Loans*

- A *Term (long-term) Loan* is a loan made by a financial institution to a business that has an initial maturity of more than one year, typically 5-12 years

Characteristics of Term Loan Agreements

12-9

- **Term Loan Agreements are the contracts under which the loans are made. Important items include:**
  - **Payment Dates**
  - **Collateral Requirements may be specified**
    - » *Secured Loan* has specific assets pledged as collateral
    - » An *Unsecured Loan* has no assets pledged as collateral
  - **Stock-Purchase Warrants**

Term Lenders

12-10

Term lenders include:

- **Commercial banks**
- **Insurance companies**
- **Pension funds**
- **Regional development companies**
- **Small Business Administration (SBA)**
- **Small Business Investment Companies (SBICs)**
- **Commercial finance companies (CFSs)**
- **Equipment manufacturers' financing subsidiaries**

12-11   ***Corporate Bonds***

- **Legal Aspects Of Corporate Bonds**
    - A *Bond Indenture* is a contract between the borrowing corporation and the bondholders, stating the conditions under which a bond has been issued
    - Common features of bond indentures include:
        - » Sinking-Fund Requirements
        - » Security Interest
    - A *Trustee* is a third party paid to protect the bondholders' interest

12-12   ***General Features Of A Bond Issue***

- **Conversion Feature**

- **Call Feature**
    - Call price - par value = call premium
    - The call feature is advantageous to the issuer

- **Stock-Purchase Warrants**

12-13   *Bond Ratings*

- **Bond Ratings reflect the riskiness of bonds as assessed by independent, third-party agencies**
- **The ratings are based upon financial ratio and cash flow analyses**
- **The higher the rating, the lower the risk (and return),and vice versa**

12-14   *Popular Types Of Bonds*

- **Traditional Bonds include:**
  - **–Debentures**
  - **–Subordinated debentures**
  - **–Income bonds**
  - **–Mortgage bonds**
  - **–Collateral trust bonds**
  - **–Equipment trust certificates**

12-15   *Popular Types Of Bonds*

Contemporary Bonds include:

- **Zero (or low) coupon bonds**
- **Junk bonds**
- **Floating rate bonds**
- **Extendable notes**
- **Putable bonds**

12-16   *International Long-Term Debt*

- Companies and governments issue debt internationally by tapping one or more of three principal financial markets. Each of these markets provides creditworthy borrowers the chance to obtain large sums of long-term financing quickly and efficiently. These markets are briefly described as follows:

12-17   ## *Eurobonds*

- A *Eurobond* is a bond issued by an international borrower and purchased by investors in countries with currency other than the currency in which the bond is denominated
- The Eurobond market has been in existence since the early 1960's and grew as American and European borrowers found that many European investors sought to hold dollar-denominated "bearer" bonds that were sheltered from taxation
- American corporations could often borrow at rates below those the federal government paid on Treasury Bonds
- The market is currently characterized by a balanced mix of European, American, and Japanese borrowers seeking "currency swap" transactions

12-18   ## *Foreign Bonds*

A foreign bond is a bond issued in a host country's financial market, in the host country's currency, by a foreign borrower

The three largest foreign bond markets are Japan, Switzerland, and the U.S., representingissuance of about $40 billion in bonds annually

12-19   *Eurocurrency Loan Market*

- The *Eurocurrency loan market* consists of a large number of international banks willing to make long-term, floating rate, hard-currency loans to international corporate and government borrowers
- Most loans are dollar-denominated and structured in the form of lines of credit
- Particularly large loans are "syndicated", i.e. pieces of the loan are sold to a large number of banks
- Approximately $500 billion in new credits are issued annually in this, the largest international long-term debt market

12-20   *Bond-Refunding Options*

- A firm that wishes to refund, or retire, a bond prior to maturity has two options
- *Serial Issues* are bonds of which a certain proportion matures each year
  - Interest rates are different at different maturities
  - The issuer cannot retire the bonds at its option
- *Exercising a Call* allows the issuer to refinance the debt, if interest rates drop, with new bonds at the lower rate
  - » Use present value techniques to determine if the PV of the interest payment and tax savings exceeds the costs of calling the old bond and issuing the new replacement bond
  - » As in capital budgeting, if the NPV (PV of annual cash flow savings - costs of calling old bond and issuing replacement bond) is greater than zero, do it

12-21   *Tax-Related Points*

- Call premiums are tax-deductible in the year of the call
- Bond discounts and premiums must be amortized over the life of the bond - discounts are treated as tax deductible expenditures, premiums as taxable income
- Flotation costs are amortized over the life of the bond and are, thus, tax-deductible expenditures
- Unamortized portions of discounts and flotation costs are deducted from pre-tax income at the time of the bond's retirement; unamortized premiums are added

12-22   *Example*

Old bond was issued 5 years ago and has 25 years until maturity with the following characteristics:

*$1,000 par value   *14% coupon interest rate

*Call price of $1,140   *Initially netted $29.1 million

*Initial flotation cost $360,000

The replacement bond will be issued with a 25 year maturity and following characteristics:

*$1,000 par   *12% coupon interest rate

*Flotation costs of $440,000

The firm has the following parameters:

* 40% tax bracket   *8% after-tax cost of debt

* 2 months of overlapping
  interest expense

Example

12-23

1.Finding the initial investment
a. Call premium
Before tax
Less: Taxes (.40 x   )
    = After-tax cost of call premium
b. Flotation cost of new bond
c. Overlapping interest
    –Before tax (.14 x 2/12 x   )
    –Less: Taxes (.40 x   )
    –= After-tax cost of overlapping interest
d. Tax savings from unamortized discount
   on old bond

e. Tax savings from unamortized flotation cost of
   old bond
Initial Investment

Example

12-24

- 2. Finding the annual cash flow saving
- Old Bond
a. Interest cost
   Before tax (.14 x   )
   Less: Taxes (.40 x   )
      = After-tax interest cost
b. Tax savings from amortization of discount

c. Tax saving from amortization of flotation cost

(1)Annual after-tax debt payment

Example

12-25

■New Bond
a. Interest Cost
Before tax (.12 x   )
Less: Taxes (.40 x   )
    = After-tax interest cost
b. Tax savings from amortization
    of flotation cost
(2)Annual after-tax debt payment
    Annual cash flow savings [(1) - (2)]
3.Finding the NPV

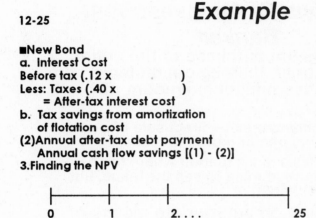

12-26

Investment Banking

- **Investment Banking plays a major role in helping firms raise both debt and equity financing**

- **Investment Bankers are financial intermediaries who purchase securities from corporations and governments for resale to the general public**

12-27
Functions Of An Investment Banker

- *Underwriting* is the purchase of the entire issue of a security, thereby guaranteeing the issuer a specified minimum amount of proceeds
    - *Private Placements* are the direct sale of a new security issue to one or more purchasers
    - *Best Efforts Basis* is a situation where the banker uses his or her resources to sell the issue, but does not underwrite it
- Advising the firm on appropriate means of financing
    - Choice of security with probable effects
    - Alternative financing arrangements
    - Merger, acquisition, and refinancing advice

12-28
Organization Of Investment Banking Activity

- Selecting an investment banker
    - Competitive Bidding: highest bidding firm wins
    - Negotiated Offering: banker is hired
- Conferring with the issuer to determine financing need and financial position
- Syndicating The Underwriting
- Forming a Selling Group

12-29 *The Security Selling Process*

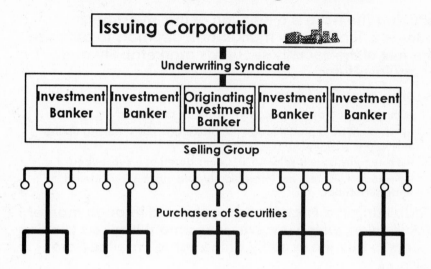

12-30 *Fulfilling Legal Requirements*

- **Registration Requirements**
  - Each registration statement must include a *prospectus* that details the firm's operating and financial position
  - A *red herring* is a statement indicating the tentative nature of an offering while under SEC review (statement is printed in red)
  - *Shelf registration* is the "warehousing" of SEC-approved securities for up to two years while the firm waits for financing need to exist or market conditions to become more favorable
- **Trading Requirements are aimed at the secondary trading of securities and are regulated by the SEC and individual state securities commissions**
- **NOTE: The state laws are sometimes called "Blue Sky Laws"**

Organization Of Investment Banking Activity

12-31

■**Pricing The Issue is a function of the investment banker's "feel" for the market and attempts to optimize the mix of the security security's marketability and financial return**

■**Distributing The Issue**

–Only after SEC approval can the issue be publicized

–Orders are accepted through the brokerage firms making up the selling group(s) and from outsiders

– If a security issue is sold out, it is considered *oversubscribed*

– If a security issue is not immediately sold out, it is considered *undersubscribed*

■**Stabilizing The Price is often achieved through** *market stabilization,* **which involves investment bankers placing orders to buy the security at the same time they are selling it**

Cost Of Investment Banking Services

12-32

• **The investment banker makes a profit by selling the security issue for more than he or she paid for it (price difference is referred to as the** *spread***)**

• **The size of the spread is a function of the administrative and underwriting costs of the issue**

– Generally, the larger the issue, the lower the overall percentage cost

– Costs are highest for common stock; lowest for bonds

12-33   *Private Placement*

- – Most commonly used for bonds or preferred stock
- – Less expensive
- – Faster since SEC approval is not necessary
- – More flexible
- Savings over public offerings are offset by:
  - – Lack of liquidity due to non-SEC registration
  - – Increased research costs
- Direct Placement Of Common Stock is sometimes achieved through:
  - – Stock Options
  - – Stock-Purchase Plans

12-34   *DISCUSSION PROBLEM*

- **Five years ago J.T. Enterprises issued bonds with the following characteristics: 12% coupon interest rate, 20 year maturity, $1,000 par, $1,050 call price, 10,000 bonds in the issue. The firm received $975 per bond and total flotation costs were $200,000. J.T. Enterprises is in the 40% tax bracket.**

12-35   *DISCUSSION PROBLEM*

• What was the total discount for the issue?

• What is the annual amount of discount amortized for the issue?

• What is the annual amount of flotation costs amortized for the issue?

• What would be the after-tax cost of calling the issue today?

12-36   *DISCUSSION PROBLEM*

• What are the tax consequences if the bond were called today?

13-1   *Common Stock and Dividend Policy*

- **The Nature Of Equity Capital**
- **Common Stock Fundamentals**
- **Stock Rights And Other Considerations**
- **Dividend Fundamentals**
- **Types Of Dividend Policies**
- **Other Forms Of Dividends**

13-2   *The Nature of Equity Capital*

- **Equity vs. Debt: Key Comparisons**

CHARACTERISTIC	EQUITY	DEBT
Ownership Rights	Voting Rights Always	Voting rights in default only
Claims on Income/Assets	Subordinate to Debt	Senior to Equity
Maturity	None	Stated
Tax treatment	No Deductions on Dividends Paid	Interest Payments areTax-Deductible

Other Points of Note

13-3

- Equity can be raised both internally (retained earnings) and externally (common and preferred stock)
- An equity base is essential to allow a firm to take optimal advantage of low-cost debt and create an optimal capital structure
- Firms with strong equity bases are more likely to survive economic downturns (recessions) since equity financing does not place the same constraints on cash flow use as does debt financing

Common Stock Fundamentals

13-4

- A common stockholder is a *residual owner*; he or she receives returns only after all other claims on the firm's income and assets have been satisfied
- Ownership can take three forms:

–Privately owned

–Closely owned

–Publicly owned

13-5   *Par Value*

Par value is a relatively useless value placed on stock in the corporate charter

- Typical par value is $1 or less
- *No Par Value* stock is assigned a value or placed on the books at its initial sale price
- Low par values are advantageous in states that base certain corporate taxes on the par value of stock

13-6   *Common Stock Terminology*

•Authorized Shares
•Outstanding Shares
•Treasury Stock
•Issued Shares

13-7

Voting Rights

- Each share of common stock entitles the owner to one vote in elections of the firm
- Because of the possibility of *hostile takeovers*, firms have issued nonvoting common stock
  - Class A stock
  - Class B stock
- *Supervoting common stock* carries more votes per share than regular common stock, thus giving its holders more control over a firm's future
- Treasury stock has no voting rights
- Votes are generally assignable
  - Proxies
  - Majority Voting
  - Cumulative Voting

13-8

Example

- If a firm has 1,000 shares outstanding and is electing three directors, and management controls 55% of the shares, all three directors backed by management will win with majority voting

Candidate	Management Votes	Candidate	Minority Votes
A	550	A-1	450
B	550	B-1	450
C	550	C-1	450

- Under cumulative voting management controls 1,650 votes (550 x 3) and minority interests control 1,350 votes (450 x 3), thus voting would result in one minority-backed director winning

Candidate	Management Votes	Candidate	Minority Votes
A	825	A-1	1,350
B	825		

13-9   *Example*

- The number of shares needed to elect a certain number of directors can be calculated as:

$$NE = \frac{O \times D}{TN+1} + 1$$

WHERE:

NE = Number of share needed to elect a certain nunber of directors

O = Total number of shares of common stock outstanding

D = Number of directors desired

TN = Total number of directors to be elected

13-10   *Example*

- Using the numbers from the previous example;
- O =   ; TN =
- To elect 1 director minority interests need at least:

NE =

- To elect 2 directors,

NE =

13-11   *Dividends*

- **Dividends can be paid in cash, stock, or merchandise**
- **Dividends are generally paid quarterly**
- **Common stock dividends cannot be paid until all claims of the government, creditors, and preferred stockholders are satisfied**

13-12   *Distribution of Earnings and Assets*

- **Distributions of Earnings and Assets are not guaranteed to common stockholders, but they can lose no more than the amount of their investment, while their potential rewards are unlimited**

13-13 *International Common Stock*

- **International Stock Issues**
  - Corporations can broaden their investor bases by listing their stock in foreign markets
  - The London, Frankfurt, and Tokyo markets are most popular with U.S. corporations
  - International stock listings also facilitate the corporation's ability to integrate itself into the local business scene and foreign acquisitions
- **American Depositary Receipts (ADRs)**
  - » Sponsored ADRs
  - » Unsponsored ADRs
- **Recent Trends**
  - Multinational equity issues are more frequent
  - Privatization of many state-owned enterprises

13-14 *Stock Rights and Other Considerations*

Stock Rights provide common stockholders' with the privilege to purchase additional shares of stock directly proportional to their number of owned shares

- **Preemptive Rights**
- **Mechanics of Rights Offerings**

13-15 *Schematic of a Rights Offering*

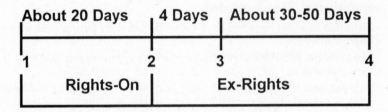

1. Announcement of a Rights Offering
2. Ex-rights day
3. Date of record
4. Expiration (final exercise) date

13-16   *Management Decisions*

• **Management must make two basic decisions:**

 –How far below current market price to set the subscription price

 –The number of rights required to purchase one share of stock

13-17   *Example*

- **The Byers Company wishes to raise $2,000,000. The current price of its stock is $53/share. The company decides upon a $50 subscription price. The company currently has 200,000 outstanding shares of common stock.**
- **Number of new shares needed to raise $2,000,000 =**

- **Number od rights required to purchase one new share at $50 =**

- **Thus, the holder of five shares of common stock will receive-five rights--one right for each share held. If the five rights are sent to the company with $50, the stockholder will receive one new share of stock**

13-18   *Value of a Right*

- **The value of a right when the stock is trading with rights can be calculated as:**

$$R_w = \frac{Mw - S}{N + 1}$$

WHERE:
- R_w =   Value of a right when stock is selling with rights
- M_w =   Market value of the stock with rights
- S =   Subscription price of the stock
- N =   Number of rights needed to purchase one share of stock

13-19

Example

- **The Byers Company stock is selling with rights for $53 per share, the subscription price is $50 per share, and it takes 5 rights to purchase one share. Thus, the value of a right is:**

R_w =

- **The value of a share of stock trading ex-rights is expected to decrease by the value of a right**

$M_e = M_w - R_w$

WHERE:

M_e = Market value of the stock trading exrights

Thus, the expected market value of Byers stock ex-rights is:

13-20

Example

- **The theoretical value of a right when the stock is trading exrights (R_e) is the same as when the stock is trading with rights and can be found with the equation**

$$R_e = \frac{M_e - S}{N}$$

13-21   *Example*

- **Using the data from the Byers example:**

$R_e =$

- **The market price of a right often differs from its theoretical value due to marketplace expectations regarding stock price behavior during the period when the rights are exercisable**

13-22   *Other Considerations*

- **Under- and Oversubscribed Offerings**
  - An undersubscribed offering is one in which the entire issue is not sold; often caused by the market price of the stock falling below its subscription price
  - To protect against undersubscription, the company and its investment banker can negotiate a *standby arrangement,* which stipulates that any unsold shares will be purchased by the investment banker
  - Most rights offerings have an *oversubscription privilege,* which allow shares not sold through the exercise of rights to be sold to interested shareholders on a pro-rata basis

13-23   *Selling Common Stock*

- **Selling common stock by means other than a rights offering include:**
  - –Stock Options for management personnel
  - –Stock-Purchase Plans as fringe benefits for employees
  - –Public or Private Placement through an investment banker

13-24 *Advantages and Disadvantages of Common Stock*

- **Advantages**
  - –Places a minimum of constraints on the firm
  - –Dividends are not required to be paid
  - –No maturity date for repayment of funds
  - –Increases the firm's borrowing power
- **Disadvantages**
  - –Potential dilution of earnings and control
  - –Potential negative signal to marketplace
  - –High cost due to high risk

13-25   *Dividend Fundamentals*

- **Recall that dividends and retained earnings come from the same "pot", i.e. net profit after taxes**
  - *Retained earnings* are the chief source of most firms' internal financing
  - Expected cash dividends are the key return variable from which owners and investors determine share price
  - Thus, dividend decisions have a direct impact upon the firm's external financing decisions

13-26   *Cash Dividend Payment Procedures*

- The firm's board of directors normally meets quarterly to evaluate financial performance and decide whether, and in what amount, dividends should be paid
- If a dividend is to be paid, the payment date and date of record are established
- The timing of a dividend payout can be illustrated as follows:

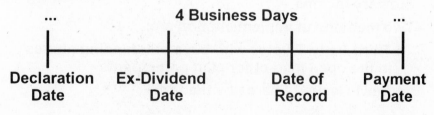

Cash Dividend Payment Procedures

13-27

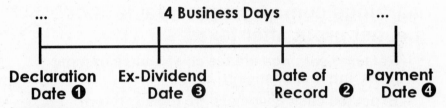

4 Business Days

Declaration Date ❶   Ex-Dividend Date ❸   Date of Record ❷   Payment Date ❹

WHERE:

❶ Declaration Date is the day the board announces the dividend

❷ Date of Record is the day on which all persons whose names are recorded as stockholders will receive the dividend

❸ Ex Dividend Date is the day on which the right to receive the dividend leaves the stock*

❹ Payment Date is the day on which dividend checks will be mailed to all stockholders of record as on the date of record

* It is common for the price of a share of stock to decline by about the value of the declared dividend on the exdividend date

13-28 *Dividend Reinvestment Plans (DRPs)*

- *Dividend Reinvestment Plans* (DRPs) enable stockholders to use dividends to acquire full and/or fractional shares of the firm's stock at little or no brokerage cost

  – Dividends that are reinvested are still taxed as ordinary income

  – Two methods of implementation are:

    » Third Party Trustee who buys outstanding shares in the open market for plan participants

    » Newly Issued Shares by the firm

13-29   *Dividend Policy Theories*

• **The *Residual Theory of Dividends* holds that dividends should be paid only if funds remain after the optimum level of capital expenditures is reached**

   – **Recall that the optimal level of capital expenditures is the intersection of the firm's WMCC curve and its investment opportunity schedule (IOS)**

   – **By determining the amount of retained earnings necessary to maintain the firm's optimal capital structure, the amount of funds, if any, left over for dividends can be calculated**

13-30   *WMCC and IOSs*

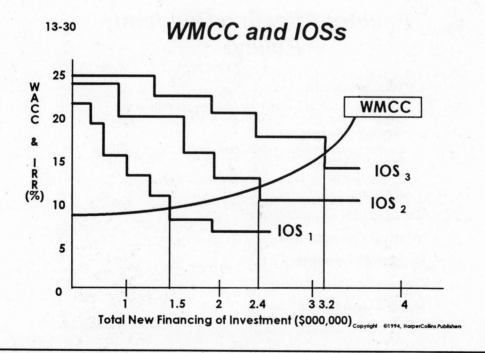

13-31   *Dividend Policy Theories*

♦ **Dividend Irrelevance Arguments (Modigliani & Miller)**
- **Dividend policy does not affect share price because:**
  - The value of the firm is a function of its earning power and the risk of its assets
    - » If dividends do affect value, it is only due to the *informational content* of dividends relative to management's earnings expectations
    - » A *clientele effect* exists which allows firms to attract shareholders whose dividend preferences match the firm's historical dividend payout patterns

♦ **Dividend Relevance Arguments (Gordon & Lintner)**
- **Dividend policy does affect share price because:**
  - Stockholders prefer current dividends due to their lower level of risk as compared to future dividends (the "bird-in-the-hand" argument)
  - Dividend payments reduce investor uncertainty (as reflected in k_s) and thereby increase stock value

13-32   *Factors Affecting Dividend Policy:*

- **Legal Constraints**
  - Cannot pay out as cash dividends any portion of the firm's "legal capital" (par value or par value plus paid-in capital in   excess of par)
  - Cannot pay out more than current and retained earnings as cash dividends
  - If insolvent or bankrupt, usually cannot pay cash dividends

- **Contractual Constraints**

- **Internal Constraints**

- **Growth Prospects**

- **Owner Considerations**

- **Market Considerations**

13-33   *Owner and Market Considerations*

- Owners generally prefer fixed or increasing dividends
- Owners prefer continuous dividends from period-to-period
- Dividend stability is seen as a *positive signal*, while dividend instability is viewed as a *negative signal*, relative to the future of the firm

13-34   *Types of Dividend Policies*

- A *dividend policy* is the firm's plan of action to be followed when dividend decisions are made
- Dividend policies must always consider two basic objectives:
  1. Maximizing owners' wealth
  2. Providing sufficient financing

13-35   *Common Dividend Policies*

- There are three common dividend policies
  - Constant-Payout-Ratio Dividend Policy
    » The dividend payout ratio is calculated as:

$$Payout\ Ratio\ =\ \frac{Dividend\ Per\ Share}{Earnings\ Per\ Share}$$

    » The firm pays out a fixed percentage of earnings each period
  - Regular Dividend Policy
  - Low-Regular-and-Extra Dividend Policy

13-36   *Other Forms of Dividends*

- **Stock Dividends**
  - *Stock Dividends* are the payment of a dividend in the form of stock (rather than cash) to existing owners
    » The transaction involves a transfer of funds from retained earnings to common stock and paid-in capital
    » The shareholders are no better off since the value of stock decreases by the same amount as the value of the dividend, leaving the market value of the shareholders' holdings unchanged
    » The firm, however, is able to retain more funds for reinvestment, which is a viable strategy for rapidly growing firms

13-37
Stock Splits

- *Stock Splits* are ways in which a firm can lower or raise the price of its stock by adjusting the number of shares belonging to each shareholder
  - The underlying reason for a stock split is to price the stock in a trading range that enhances its marketability
  - The transaction involves an adjustment in the number of outstanding shares of stock and the stock's par value
  - Most splits seek to lower share price, such as a 2-for-1 split, after which each shareholder owns twice as many shares of stock with a par value equal to its value prior to the split
  - To raise share price the firm can use a reverse stock split, after which each shareholder owns twice as many shares of stock with a par value equal to half its value prior to the split

13-38
Stock Repurchases

- *Stock Repurchases* are purchasing by firms of outstanding shares of their own common stock in the marketplace
- Motives for repurchase include:
  - Obtaining shares for acquisitions
  - Obtaining shares for employee stock option plans
  - Retiring outstanding shares to distribute cash to owners and increase EPS
- The transaction involves a reduction of cash, an addition to a contra capital account known as "treasury stock", and a corresponding reduction in stockholders' equity

13-39   *Stock Repurchases*

- **The advantages of a repurchase to the stockholders are:**
  - –Excess cash is distributed to the owners
  - –Earnings per share increase (assuming earnings remain constant) which usually leads to an increase in share price
  - –If share price increases, shareholder wealth increases without having to pay taxes on the increase until the stock is sold

13-40   *Stock Repurchases*

- **The basic methods of repurchase include:**
  - –Open Market Purchase
  - –Tender Offer
  - –Purchase on a Negotiated Basis

13-41   *DISCUSSION PROBLEM*

- **The Ellis Company's equity accounts are shown below:**

Common stock ($1 par; 500,000 shares)	$ 500,000
Paid-in capital in excess of par	1,500,000
Retained earnings	1,000,000
Total stockholder's equity	$3,000,000

- **If the board of directors declares a 20% stock dividend, what   will the resulting changes be in the equity accounts? (current   share price =$7)**

13-42   *SOLUTION*

- Number of new shares issued =
- Total needed to transfer from retained earnings =

- New equity account balances:

Common stock
Paid-in capital in excess of par
Retained earnings
  Total stockholder's equity

13-43   ## DISCUSSION PROBLEM

- The Nissa Corporation stock is currently trading at $95/share. The firm is concerned that the price is too high for normal trading activity to occur, so it declared a 2-for-1 stock split. Given the pre-split equity accounts below, show the effect of the stock split on these accounts

Pre-split Equity Account:

Common stock

($4 par; 1,000,000 shares)	$ 4,000,000
Paid-in capital in excess of par	10,000,000
Retained earnings	6,000,000
Total stockholder's equity	$20,000,000

13-44   ## SOLUTION

- Post-split Equity Account:

13-45   *DISCUSSION PROBLEM*

- **If you owned 10,000 shares of Ellis Company stock prior to the stock dividend, show that the stock dividend did not change your ownership position, assuming the company's net income is $1,000,000.**

- **SOLUTION**

Preferred Stock, Leasing, Convertibles, Warrants, and Options

14-1

- # Preferred Stock
- # Leasing
- # Convertible Securities
- # Stock-Purchase Warrants
- # Options

14-2   ## Prefered Stock

- **Preferred Stock is sometimes known as a "hybrid" security because it has some features typical of debt and other features typical of equity**
  - Basic types of preferred stock include:
    - » Par-Value
    - » No-Par
  - Preferred stock is issued most often by public utilities, by acquiring firms in mergers, and by firms experiencing losses and in need of financing

14-3   *Basic Rights of Preferred Stockholders*

- **Preference over common stockholders relative to:**
  - Distribution of earnings
  - Distribution of assets

- **Voting rights under certain limited conditions**

14-4   *Features of Preferred Stock*

- **Restrictive covenants**
- **Cumulation**
- **Participation**
- **Call Feature**
- **Conversion Feature**

14-5 *Special Types of Preferred Stock*

- **Adjustable-rate (or floating rate) preferred stock (ARPS)**
  - Variable dividend rate tied to interest rates on government securities
  - Can be sold at initially lower dividend rates
- **Payment-in-kind (PIK) preferred stock**
  - Doesn't pay cash dividends, but rather pays in additional shares of preferred stock
  - Used primarily to finance takeovers
  - Not a major corporate financing tool

14-6 *Advantages and Disadvantages of Preferred Stock*

- **Advantages include:**
  - Its existence increases the firm's financial leverage
  - It is more flexible than debt when it comes to missing an annual payment
  - It is useful for corporate restructuring
- **Disadvantages include:**
  - Its senior status to common stockholders jeopardizes common stockholders' returns
  - Its cost is generally greater than that of debt financing
  - It is sometimes difficult to sell since dividends can be passed (unpaid) and returns are generally fixed

14-7   *Leasing*

- A *Lease* is a contractual agreement by which an owner of assets (the lessor) allows another party (the lessee) to use the assets for a specific period of time in return for   periodic cash payments

- A lease is best viewed as a form of debt financing since it entails fixed-payment obligations that are tax-deductible

14-8   *Basic Types of Leases:*

- **Operating Leases**
  - Most operating leases are for a period of time less   than the asset's useful economic life
  - Computers, office copiers, and motor vehicles are   examples of assets commonly leased in this manner
  - At the end of the lease the lessee returns the asset   to the lessor who may lease it again or sell it outright

- **Financial (or Capital)Leases**
  - Total payments over the lease period are greater   than the lessor's initial cost
  - Land, buildings, and equipment are examples of   assets commonly leased in this manner
  - At the end of the lease, ownership of the asset is   often transferred from the lessor to the lessee, or   the lessee has an option to purchase it at a "prespecified price"

14-9   *Leasing Arrangements:*

• Direct Lease
• Sale-Leaseback Arrangement
• Leveraged Lease

14-10   *Lease Contract*

The Lease Contract includes the following items:

- Description of the leased assets
- Duration of lease
- Cancellation provisions, if any
- Lease payment amounts and dates
- Maintenance provisions, if any
- Renewal features, if any
- Purchase options, if any
- Penalties for missing payments

14-11   *The Lease-Versus-Purchase Decision*

- **The Lease-Versus-Purchase-Decision addresses the issue of whether the firm is better off leasing an asset or buying the asset given three basic choices:**
  - **Lease the asset(s)**
  - **Borrow funds to purchase the asset(s)**
  - **Use available liquid resources to purchase the asset(s)**

14-12   *Lease-Versus-Purchase Decisions*

- **Steps involved in lease-versus-purchase analysis**

❶ **Determine the after-tax cash outflow for each year under the lease alternative**

❷ **Determine the after-tax cash outflows for each year under the purchase alternative**

❸ **Calculate the present value of the cash outflows under each alternative using the after-tax cost of debt as the discount rate**

❹ **Choose the alternative with the lowest present value of cash outflows from Step 3**

14-13   *Example*

- **The Pamela Corporation has a choice of purchasing a piece of equipment for $50,000 using a 10%, six-year loan or leasing the equipment for a six-year period with an annual (end-of-year) lease payment of $10,000. If the company purchases the equipment, it will pay $750 per year in expenses for a maintenance contract. The equipment will be depreciated under MACRS guidelines for a 5-year asset. If the company leases the equipment, it incurs no maintenance costs and can purchase the asset for $10,000 at the termination of the lease. Given that the Pamela Corporation has a marginal tax rate of 40%, which alternative should be chosen?**

14-14   *Example*

- **Step 1**

After-tax outflows under leasing alternative:

Year Payment x (1-.40) = After-tax Cash Flows

1

2

3

4

5

6

14-15

Example

- **Step 2**

After-tax outflows under purchase alternative:

a. Amortization Schedule of Loan

Year Payment Interest Principal Outstanding Principal

1

2

3

4

5

6

14-16

Example

b. Tax-Deductible Outflows

Year	Loan Payment (1)	Maintenance (2)	Deprec. (3)	Int. (4)	Total Deductions [(2)+(3)+(4)] (5)	Tax Shields [(5)x.4] (6)	After-Tax Cash Outflows [(1)+(2)-(6)] (7)
1							
2							
3							
4							
5							
6							

14-17

Example

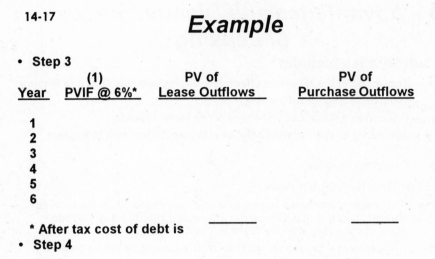

- Step 3

Year	(1) PVIF @ 6%*	PV of Lease Outflows	PV of Purchase Outflows
1			
2			
3			
4			
5			
6			

* After tax cost of debt is

- Step 4

14-18 ## *Effects of Leasing on Future Financing*

- **FASB Standard No. 13 requires explicit disclosure of financial lease arrangements as an asset and corresponding liability on the firm's balance sheet**

- **FASB Standard No. 13 requires details of operating lease arrangements to be disclosed in footnotes to financial statements**

- **Financial ratio analyses performed on the lessee's balance sheet thus reflect its true financial status**

14-19 *Advantages and Disadvantages of Leasing*

- **Advantages include:**
  - The ability of the lessee to effectively depreciate land that it is leasing
  - 100% financing for the lessee
  - Protection against obsolescence of the leased assets
  - Avoidance of the restrictive covenants associated with long-term loans
  - Financing flexibility

- **Disadvantages include:**
  - The lessee sometimes pays a rate of return higher than the cost of borrowing to purchase the asset The lessor realizes any salvage value of the asset at the termination of the lease
  - The lessee may be prohibited from making improve ments to the asset without the lessor's approval

14-20

Convertible Securities

• There are two types of convertible securities:
–Convertible Bonds
–Convertible Preferred Stock

14-21   **General Features of Convertibles**

- The *Conversion Ratio* is the number of shares of common stock that can be received in exchange for each convertible security
- The *Conversion Price* is the per share common stock price at which the exchange effectively takes place

14-22   *Example*

- If a firm has a bond with a $1,000 par value that is convertible at $40 per share of common stock, the conversion ratio =

_____ =

- If the firm had stated the conversion ratio at 20, the conversion price =

_____ =

14-23   *Example*

- The *Conversion Period* is a limited time within which a security may be exchanged for common stock
- The *Conversion Value* is the market value of the security based upon the conversion ratio times the current market price of the firm's common stock
- The Effects on Earnings of convertible securities are as follows:
  - Firms must report *Primary EPS*, treating all contingent securities that derive their value from their conversion privileges or common stock characteristics as common stock
  - Firms must report *Fully Diluted EPS* treating all contingent securities as common stock

14-24 *Financing With Convertibles*

- Motives for using convertibles include:
  - It is a deferred sale of common stock that decreases   the dilution of both ownership and earnings
  - They can be used as a "sweetener" for financing
  - They can be sold at a lower interest rate than nonconvertibles
  - They have far fewer restrictive covenants than nonconvertibles
  - It provides a temporarily cheap source of funds (assuming bonds) for financing projects
- Most convertibles have a call feature that enables the issuer to force conversion when the price of the common stock rises above the conversion price
- Sometimes the price of common stock does not reach a level sufficient to stimulate conversion, and the security is known as an *overhanging issue*

14-25   ## *Determining the Value of a Convertible Bond*

- **There are three values associated with a convertible bond:**
  - *Straight Bond Value* is the price at which the bond would sell in the market without the conversion feature
  - The *Conversion Value* is, once again, the product of the current market price of stock times the conversion ratio of the bond
  - The *Market Value* is the straight or conversion value plus a market premium based upon future (expected) stock price movements that will enhance the value of the conversion feature

14-26

Example

- **The Duncan Company sold a $1,000 par value, 20-year convertible   bond with a 12% coupon.   A straight bond would have been sold with a 14% coupon.   The conversion ratio is 20**

  - **Straight Bond Value**

  - **Conversion Value at various market prices of stock**

  Stock Price   Conversion Value

14-27

Values and Market Premium

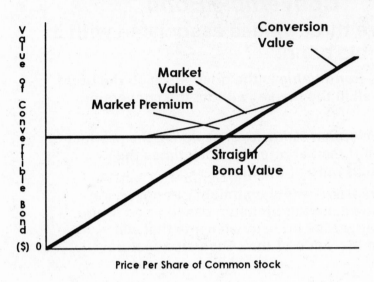

Price Per Share of Common Stock

14-28

Stock-Purchase Warrants

- Warrants are usually detachable
- Warrants are often added to a large debt issue as "sweeteners" to enhance the marketability of the issue
- Exercise price
- Warrants usually have a limited life of about 10 years or less
- Warrants are usually detachable and trade on the securities exchanges
- Warrants differ from rights
- Warrants differ from convertibles

14-29

The Implied Price of an Attached Warrant

- To determine the implied price of an attached warrant, the implied price of *all* warrants attached to a bond must be determined

Implied price of all warrants = price of bond with warrants attached - the straight   bond value
(of similar-risk   bonds)

- The impled price of a single warrant is the implied price of all warrants divided by the number of warrants attached to each bond

14-30

The Value of Warrants

- A warrant has a theoretical value at any point in time prior to its expiration date
- The theoretical value of a warrant can be calculated as:

$TVW = (P_o - E) \times N$

- WHERE:

TVW =   Theoretical value of a warrant

P_o =   Current market price of one share of common stock

E =   Exercise price of the warrant

N =   Number of shares of common stock

obtainable with one warrant

14-31

Example

- Wong Electronics has outstanding warrants exercisable at $40/share that entitle holders to purchase three shares of common stock per warrant. If the firm's common stock is currently selling for $45/share, the TVW =

    TVW =

- The market value of a warrant is generally greater than its theoretical value; the difference, known as the warrant premium is due to investor expectations and leverage opportunities relative to directly purchasing the common stock

14-32 ## *Values and Warrant Premium*

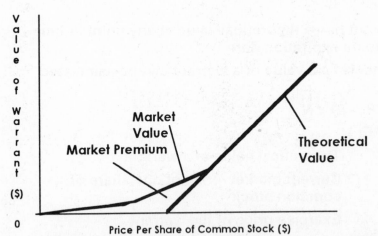

- The use of warrants by investors is more risky than purchasing stock

14-33

Options

- *Options* are instruments that provide their holders with an opportunity to purchase or sell a specified asset at a stated price on or before a set expiration date
- Both rights and warrants are forms of options
- Options on common stock receive a great deal of attention

14-34

Calls and Puts

- **More common forms of options on common stock are "calls" and "puts"**
  - **–Call option; an option to buy**
  - **–Put option; an option to sell**
  - **–Striking price**

14-35 *How the Options Markets Work*

- **Options may be transacted in two ways:**
  - With the help of a stockbroker through a call and   put options dealer
  - Through brokerage or outside traders on one of   several organized options exchanges such as the Chicago Board Options Exchange (CBOE)

14-36 *Logic of Options Trading*

- **The logic underlying call option trading is that if an investor expects the market price of a particular stock to rise more than enough to cover the cost of   the option, the investor will purchase a call option**

14-37

Example

- Susan Sanchez has purchased a three-month call option on Stockton Company stock for $300, with a striking price of $35. To cover the cost of the option (ignoring brokerage fees) Stockton stock must rise to $38/share [100 shares x ($38 - $35) = $300]. If the stock price rises to $40/share, Susan will make:

- If the price of stock never rises above the strike price, Susan

- If the price of stock rises to a point between the strike price and $38, Susan

- If an investor feels the market price of a particular stock will decline over the life of an option, the investor will purchase a *put option*

- Investors often purchase put options on shares of stock they actually own in order to protect against losing a gain already earned or to protect against a potential loss

14-38 # *Role of Call and Put Options in Managerial Finance*

- Options have no direct, and very little indirect, impact upon the fund-raising activities of a firm's financial manager

- Since options are issued by investors and not businesses they are not a source of financing to the firm

- Buyers of options have no voting rights, therefore, no say in the firm's management

14-39   ## *Using Options to Hedge Foreign Currency Exposures*

- The Philadelphia Stock Exchange (PHLX) offers exchange-traded options contracts on the Canadian dollar, Japanese yen, and several major European currencies

- Options allow an American company making a transaction denominated in a foreign currency to protect against the risk of adverse exchange rate movements while still preserving the possibility of profiting if exchange rate movement are favorable

- One difficulty, however, is matching the size of the transaction to the size of the option(s) purchased since a perfect match is relatively rare

14-40   ## *DISCUSSION PROBLEMS*

- The Nissa Corporation has a $1000 par, 15-year, 9% convertible bond outstanding. The bond was issued 5 years ago and is convertible into 40 shares of common stock. Similar-risk bonds that are nonconvertible sold at an 11% coupon rate.

A. What is the minimum the Nissa bonds are worth?

- SOLUTION

14-41   *DISCUSSION PROBLEM*

- If Nissa stock is currently selling for $27.50/share, what is the conversion value of the bond?

- SOLUTION

14-42   *DISCUSSION PROBLEM*

- At what common stock price will the conversion value equal the straight bond value

- SOLUTION

$$P_o =$$

14-43   **DISCUSSION PROBLEM**

- The Reyes Company has outstanding warrants with a theoretical value of $21. If the exercise price is $33/share and the current price of Reyes stock is $36/share, how many shares of stock does each warrant entitle its holder to purchase?

- SOLUTION

14-44   **DISCUSSION PROBLEM**

- Brokers for the Samantha Corporation are asking $1,000 for the firm's $1,000 par, 20 year bonds paying an 8.5% coupon rate annually and having 10 warrants attached for the purchase of common stock. Similar risk straight bonds are currently carrying a coupon rate of 11%. If the market value of the warrant is $21, what is the warrant premium?

- SOLUTION

1. Find the value of a similar risk straight bond
       B_o =

2. Find implied value of all warrants

3. Find the implied value of a single warrant

4. Find the warrant premium

¹⁵⁻¹ *Financial Planning*

- **The Financial Planning Process**
- **Cash Planning: Cash Budgets**
- **Profit Planning: Pro Forma Statement Fundamentals**
- **Preparing The Pro Forma Income Statement**
- **Preparing The Pro Forma Balance Sheet**
- **Evaluation Of Pro Forma Statements**

¹⁵⁻² *The Financial Planning Process*

- **Financial planning provides important assistance to the firm's management in guiding, coordinating, and controlling the firm's actions toward achieving its objectives**
- **The process begins with the long-term (strategic) financial plans that guide the formulation of short-term (operating) financial plans and budgets**
- **The short-term plans and budgets are used to implement the firm's long-term strategic objectives**

15-3 *Long-Term (Strategic) Financial Plans*

- Are planned long-term financial actions and their anticipated outcomes
- Typically cover a two-to-ten-year planning horizon
- Consider fixed-asset outlays, research and development activities, marketing and product development actions, capital structure, and major sources of financing
- Also consider the termination or downsizing of existing activities and products, along with the repayment of outstanding debt

15-4   *Short-Term (Operating) Financial Plans*

- Are planned short-term financial actions and their anticipated outcomes
- Typically cover a period of one to two years
- Use sales forecasts and certain operating and financial data as key inputs
- Produce operating budgets, the cash budget, and pro forma financial statements

15-5   *Short Term Financial Planning*

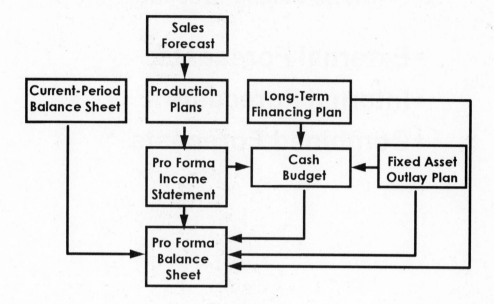

15-6   *Cash Planning: Cash Budgets*

- Since many sales do not immediately generate cash, and many firms face seasonal and other sales fluctuations, planning for the availability of cash is important
- A *Cash Budget* is a forecast of the firm's inflows and outflows of cash over a certain (short-term) period of time
  - A typical cash budget is divided into monthly intervals and covers one year
  - The actual number and type of intervals depend on the nature of the business
  - Of most importance to the financial manager are the projected cash surpluses and shortages

15-7   *The Sales Forecast*

- **External Forecasts**
- **Internal Forecasts**
- **Combined Forecasts**

15-8   *Preparing The Cash Budget*

- The general format of a cash budget
- *Cash Receipts* are the inflows of cash during a given period, notably cash sales, collections of accounts receivable, and other (non-sales-related) inflows
  - It is often helpful to evaluate the historical pattern of sales by pertinent time interval

15-9

Example

- **For a firm interested in a monthly cash budget, it can construct a table from its historical sales data detailing percentages of annual monthly sales**

Month	Historical % of Sales	Actual Last Year	Projected
January	5%	$ 20,000	---
February	12%	$ 48,000	---
	100%	$400,000	Forecast Sales

- **If sales are projected to be $450,000 next year, the January projected sales total will be $22,500 (.05 x $450,000)**
- **It is also helpful to create an aging schedule for sales showing the collection pattern of accounts receivable**

15-10

Example

Payment	% of Customers Paying
In cash	25%
Within month of sale	15
31-60 days	25
61-90 days	15
-	--
-	--
	100%

- **With the information from the two tables above, a schedule of cash receipts can be constructed**

15-11   *Cash Budget*

- *Cash Disbursements* are the outflows of cash during a given period, notably cash purchases, payments of accounts payable, rent, wages and salaries, taxes, loan payments, etc.
- Net Cash Flow, Ending Cash, Financing, and Excess Cash
  - Net Cash Flow
  - Ending Cash
  - Subtracting a budget period's minimum cash balance (as set by the financial manager) from that period's ending cash balance results in one of two possible figures:
    » If the ending cash balance exceeds the minimum cash balance, the firm has Excess Cash to invest
    » If the ending cash balance is less than the minimum cash balance, the firm requires short-term Financing

15-12 *Evaluating The Cash Budget*

- The cash budget shows the period(s) in which a cash flow problem could arise for the firm
- The cash budget allows management time to arrange a line of credit in preparation for cash shortages
- The cash budget allows management to anticipate potential cash surpluses available for investment
- Management needs to remember that the cash budget is only an estimate of inflows and outflows of cash and must be monitored each budget period

15-13 Coping With Uncertainty In The Cash Budget

- **A firm can prepare a series of cash budgets, each based on a different set of assumptions**

- **A firm can create a computer simulation to develop a probability distribution of its monthly ending cash flows**

15-14 Cash Flow Within The Month

- **Some firms need to track cash on a daily basis due to their patterns of actual cash receipts and disbursements**
  - It is not uncommon for a firm to project excess cash for a particular month, but face cash shortages during the month
  - A firm can attempt to better synchronize its disbursements with its receipts by choosing vendors with billing cycles more closely matched to cash receipt patterns of the firm

- **The greater the variability of cash flows from day-to-day, the greater the attention required**

Profit Planning: Pro Forma Statement Fundamentals

15-15

- **Pro Forma Statements are projected financial statements**
- **The most popular approaches are based on the belief that a firm's historical financial relationships can be used to predict its financial activities over the planning horizon (typically one year)**
- **While their primary purpose is for internal planning, pro forma statements may be required by prospective creditors**

15-16

Inputs Required

The inputs required include:

- **Past year's financial statements**
- **Coming year's sales forecast**
- **An understanding of the firm's accounts that have, and do not have, a measurable relationship to sales**

15-17   *Preparing the Pro-Forma Income Statement*

- The *Percent-of-Sales Method* is used to develop the pro forma income statement by expressing the cost of goods sold, operating expenses, and interest expense as a percentage of projected sales
- Preparing a *common-size income statement* for the preceding year is a helpful beginning to the process
- It is more realistic to break the firm's costs and expenses into fixed and variable components and make the forecast using these relationships
- This approach is simplistic since all variable costs and expenses are assumed to change by the same percentage that sales is predicted to change

Percentage change = [(sales forecast/last year's sales)-1]X 100

15-18 *Pro Forma Income Statement Revisions*

- **The first pro forma income statement may have to be revised as new information affecting certain accounts is received**
  - Regression analysis techniques can be used to determine the fixed and variable nature of each cost
  - Common stock dividends are likely to change, as is interest expense, due to changes in levels of activity and profitability

15-19 *Preparing the Pro-Forma balance Sheet*

- The *Judgmental Approach* is used to develop the pro forma balance sheet by calculating some balance sheet accounts while estimating others, and using the firm's (additionally needed) *external funds required* as a balancing figure
- The goal is to determine how much external funds will be required to support the firm's projected activity level
- The inputs to the procedure include:
  - 1. Prior period balance sheet
  - 2. Pro forma income statement
  - 3. Assumptions with regard to particular balance sheet accounts and their relationships to sales

15-20 *The Procedure*

The procedure is as follows:
- Determine increases in asset accounts
  - 1. Adjust those accounts that change directly with sales by the same percentage change that is projected for sales
  - 2. Estimate changes in other asset accounts
- Determine increases in liability accounts in the same manner as the increases in assets were determined, noting that many liability accounts will remain unchanged
- Determine changes in equity accounts, especially noting the increase in retained earnings calculated on the pro forma income statement
- Subtract the total of estimated liabilities and equity from the estimated total assets
  - 1. If positive, the difference is the "plug" figure "external funds required" and the firm must develop a financing plan to raise that much external funding
  - 2. If negative, the firm will have excess funds to repay debt, repurchase stock, or pay dividends

15-21   *Evaluation of Pro-Forma Statements*

- **Even with the proliferation and wide acceptance of spreadsheet software and personal computers, the popularity of the simplified approaches to developing pro forma statements is likely to remain strong**

15-22   *Weaknesses Of Simplified Approaches*

- **Assuming that the past is a good predictor of the future**

- **Assuming that certain variables can be forced to take on certain "desired" values**

15-23 *Using Pro Forma Statements*

- Aside from estimating the need for any external financing, pro forma statements are useful for:
  - Analyzing planned sources and use of funds
  - Analyzing profitability and overall financial performance
  - Performing pro forma ratio analysis
  - Generating the lead time to prepare for the sale of debt or equity securities
  - Allowing adjustments to be made to operating plans in anticipation of future events "predicted" by pro forma analysis

15-24 *DISCUSSION PROBLEMS*

The Burian Company has estimated next year's increase in asset accounts to be $125,000. Liability accounts are expected to increase by $50,000 and Burian expects to pay out $25,000 in dividends on net profits of $60,000. How much, if any, additional external financing will Burian need given these expectations

15-25

SOLUTION

Retained earnings will increase by

Expected Increases

Assets   Liabilities & Equity

External financing required =

15-26

DISCUSSION PROBLEM

Mario & Mark, Inc. has projected its requirement for funds next year to be $15,000. The pro forma balance sheet summaries are as follows:

Current Assets	$30,000	Current Liabilities	$12,000
Fixed Assets	60,000	Long-Term Debt	20,000
		Common Equity	43,000
	$90,000		$75,000

Management would like to finance the $15,000 shortfall ($90,000 - $75,000) primarily with short- term borrowing, but will borrow long-term and sell common stock if necessary. A restriction in the indenture in their last bond issue limits M & M's ability to borrow. The indenture requires a minimum current ratio of 2.25 and a maximum debt ratio of .40. Given these restrictions, create a financing plan for Mario & Mark, Inc.

15-27   *SOLUTION*

- **Current ratio minimum is 2.25, so determine the maximum short-term borrowing possible.**

- **Debt ratio maximum is .40, so, determine the maximum total borrowing**

- **Determine equity financing needed**

- **Financing Plan:**   Short-Term Borrowing
                    Long-Term Borrowing
                    Common Stock
                       Total

16-1 **Net Working Capital and Short-Term Financing**

- **Net Working Capital Fundamentals**
- **Net Working Capital Strategies**
- **Spontaneous Sources Of Short-Term Financing**
- **Unsecured Sources Of Short-Term Loans**
- **Secured Sources Of Short-Term Loans**

16-2 **Net Working Capital**

- **Short-Term Financial Management** involves the management of the firm's current assets and current liabilities
  - ■This is one of the most important and time-consuming activities of the financial manager
  - ■There is a constant need to balance profitability and risk while attempting to maximize owner wealth
    - ■Too high an investment in current assets reduces profitability
    - ■Too low an investment in current assets exposes the firm to the risk of not meeting current obligations
    - ■Both situations can lead to lower firm value

16-3   *Net Working Capital*

- **Net Working Capital is the difference between current assets and current liabilities**
  - It is also the portion of current assets being financed by long-term funds
  - The firm's *operating cycle*, which is the ongoing transformation of a firm's working capital from cash to inventory to receivables to cash, is an important component of short-term financial management
  - The firm's current liabilities include all obligations that will come due and must be paid within one year
  - Net working capital is ideally positive, but can be negative
  - The more predictable a firm's cash inflows, the less net working capital it needs

The Tradeoff Between
16-4   *Profitability and Risk*

- *Profitability* is the relationship between revenues and costs generated by using the firm's assets in productive activities
- To increase profitability, a firm must:
  - Increase revenue; Decrease costs; Some combination of both
- Risk, in the current context, refers to the probability that a firm will be unable to pay its bills as they come due
- Other important assumptions include:
  - Fixed assets earn a higher return than current assets
  - Long-term financing is more expensive than current-liability financing
  - The nearer an asset is to cash, the less risky it is
- Changes in current assets can be examined by using the ratio of current assets to total assets
- Changes in current liabilities can be examined using the ratio of current liabilities to total assets

16-5 *Effects of Changing Ratios on Profits and Risk*

Ratio	Change in ratio	Effect on profit	Effect on risk
<u>Current assets</u> Total assets	Increase Decrease	Decrease Increase	Decrease Increase
<u>Current liabilities</u> Total assets	Increase Decrease	Increase Decrease	Increase Decrease

Net Working Capital Strategies

16-6

- **A fundamental decision is to what extent current liabilities   will be used to finance current assets**
- **Current liabilities are limited, or constrained, as follows:**
  - **Accounts payable are limited by the dollar amount of purchases**
  - **Accruals are limited by the dollar amounts of accrued liabilities**
  - **Notes payable and commercial paper are limited by the amount of seasonal borrowing considered acceptable by lenders**

16-7   *The Firm's Financing Need*

The firm's financing need can be separated into two components

- *Permanent Need* supports the firm's fixed assets plus the permanent portion of the firm's current assets
- *Seasonal Need* supports the temporary current assets, which vary over the year

Estimated Funds for Nicholson Company

16-8

Month	Current assets (1)	Fixed assets (2)	Total assets [(1)+(2)] (3)	Permanent funds requirement (4)	Seasonal funds requirement [(3)-(4)] (5)
January	$4,000	$13,000	$17,000	$ 13,800	$3,200
February	3,000	13,000	16,000	13,800	2,300
March	2,000	13,000	15,000	13,800	1,200
April	1,000	13,000	14,000	13,800	200
May	800	13,000	13,800	13,800	0
June	1,500	13,000	14,500	13,800	700
July	3,000	13,000	16,000	13,800	2,200
August	3,700	13,000	16,700	13,800	2,900
September	4,000	13,000	17,000	13,800	3,200
October	5,000	13,000	18,000	13,800	4,200
November	3,000	13,000	16,000	13,800	2,200
December	2,000	13,000	15,000	13,800	1,200
Monthly average				$13,800	$1,950

16-9   *An Aggressive Financing Strategy*

- An *aggressive financing strategy* uses short-term funds to finance all of a firm's seasonal needs and, perhaps, a portion of its permanent needs
- Cost Considerations
    - Lowers cost by using as much of the cheaper short-term financing as is possible
    - Should lead to high profitability
- Risk Considerations
    - High Risk since NWC is minimized
    - May be difficult to obtain long-term funds in an emergency

16-10   *Conservative Financing Strategy*

- A *conservative financing strategy* uses long-term funds to finance all of a firm's projected needs and uses short-term   funds only in emergencies
- In a pure sense this is hard to implement since it is nearly impossible to avoid the use of "spontaneous" short-term financing sources such as accounts payable and accruals
- Cost Considerations
    - Higher cost since long-term financing is more expensive and not actually needed throughout the period during which the firm pays interest on it
    - Should lead to low profitability

16-11   *Conservative Financing Strategy*

•Risk considerations:

–Low Risk since NWC is maximized

–Sufficient short-term borrowing capacity should be readily available in an emergency

16-12   *Conservative Versus Aggressive Strategy*

- Most firms operate somewhere between the high-profit, high-risk aggressive strategy and the low-profit, low-risk conservative strategy

- A commonly cited strategy is a "tradeoff approach" that balances the profit and risk in a fashion consistent with the financial managers' (i.e., the firms) risk preference

16-13   *Spontaneous Sources of Short-Term Financing*

- **Spontaneous sources of financing arise from the normal operations of the firm, most notably accounts payable and accruals**
- **These spontaneous financing sources also:**
  - **Have no explicit costs attached to them**
  - **Are unsecured, i.e. do not require the pledge of specific assets as collateral**

16-14   *Accounts Payable*

- **Credit Terms associated with accounts payable:**
  - *Credit Period* is the number of days until full payment is due
  - *Cash Discount* is a percentage deduction from the purchase price if the buyer pays within a specified shorter time period than the credit period
  - *Cash Discount Period* is the number of days after the beginning of the credit period during which the cash discount is attainable
  - *Beginning of the Credit Period* is when the credit period begins as stated by the supplier, most often
    - » Date of Invoice
    - » End of Month (EOM)

16-15

Example

**The Simpson Corporation made two purchases
-- one on September 10 and the other on
September 20-- from each of two suppliers
offering the following terms:**

2/10 net 30 End of Month

vs.

2/10 net 30 Date of Invoice

Payment Dates for the Simpson Corporation Given Various Assumptions

16-16

Beginning of Credit period	SEPTEMBER 10 PURCHASE		SEPTEMBER 20 PURCHASE	
	Discount taken	Net amount paid	Discount taken	Net amount paid
Date of invoice	Sept. 20	Oct. 10	Sept. 30	Oct. 20
End of Month	Oct. 10	Oct. 30	Oct. 10	Oct. 30

16-17
Analyzing Credit Terms

- Purchasers should carefully analyze the terms of credit offered by suppliers in order to determine the optimal trade credit strategy
  - Taking the Cash Discount
    - » Pay on the last day of the discount period
    - » Amount paid equals cost minus discount
  - Giving up the Cash Discount
    - » Pay entire amount on the last day of the credit period
    - » There is an implicit cost of giving up the cash discount, calculated as:

$$\text{Cost of giving up cash discount} = \frac{CD}{100\% - CD} \times \frac{360}{N}$$

WHERE:

CD = Stated cash discount in percentage terms

N = Number of days payment can be delayed by giving up the cash discount

16-18
Example

- **A firm makes a $1,000 purchase on February 27 from a supplier with the terms 2/10 net 30 EOM.**

If the firm pays by March 10, it will receive a $20 discount (2% x $1,000) and, thus, pay $980

After March 10, the firm must pay the entire $1,000 and the implicit cost of giving up the cash discount is:

Using the Cost of Giving up a Cash Discount in Decision Making

16-19

- **It is prudent for the financial manager to compute the cost of giving up the cash discount for each of the firm's suppliers**

Cash Discounts and Associated Costs for Mason Products

16-20

Supplier	Credit terms	Approximate cost of giving up cash discount
A	1/10 net 30 EOM	36.0%
B	1/10 net 55 EOM	8.0
C	3/20 net 70 EOM	21.6
D	4/10 net 60 EOM	28.8

By comparing the above costs with the current rate of interest being charged by the firm's bank for short-term funds, the financial manager can develop an accounts payable strategy for each supplier

Effects of Stretching Accounts Payable

16-21

- A firm can reduce its cost of giving up a cash discount by stretching accounts payable, or paying its bills as late as possible without damaging its credit rating

- This strategy, however, raises an important ethical issue since it causes the firm to violate the agreement it entered with its supplier when it purchased the merchandise. This issue may offset its financial attractiveness

16-22

Example

- We saw that with terms of 2/10 net 30 EOM the cost of giving up the cash discount was 36.7%. If the supplier allowed the firm to pay in 70 days without damaging its credit rating, the cost of giving up the discount is reduced to:

16-23
Accruals

- *Accruals*, which are liabilities for services received for which payment has yet to be made, are another source of spontaneous short-term financing
- The most common items accrued are wages and taxes
- The strategy is to delay payment of accrued items as much as possible, since they are in effect interest-free loans from the parties to whom the payments are owed

Unsecured Sources of Short-Term Loans
16-24

- **The two major sources of unsecured short-term loans are commercial banks and commercial paper**
  - Each is negotiated by the financial manager
  - Bank loans are more popular since they are more readily available to firms of all sizes

16-25

Bank Loans

- **Loan Interest Rates**
  - *Prime Rate of Interest* is the rate upon which all other rates are based
    - » The bank's best business borrowers may obtain loans at, or sometimes below, prime
    - » Most loans are at prime plus a risk-based increment
      - Fixed-Rate Loan
      - Floating-Rate Loan
  - **Method of Computing Interest**
    - » Interest *paid at maturity* of the loan
      - For a loan upon which interest is paid at maturity, the effective interest rate is calculated as:

$$\frac{\text{\$ Interest Paid}}{\text{Amount Borrowed}}$$

    - » *Paid in advance*, creating a discount loan
      - For a discount loan the effective interest rate is calculated as:

$$\frac{\text{\$ Interest Paid}}{\text{Amount Borrowed - Interest}}$$

16-26

Example

- **If a firm needs to borrow $15,000 for one year and the bank has a stated rate of interest of 12%, the firm will pay:**

  The *effective interest rate* for each alternative is:

  At maturity:

  In advance:

16-27 *Notes and Lines of Credit*

- *Single-Payment Notes* are one-shot loans, 30 days to 9 months in maturity, with interest tied to the prime rate
- *Lines of Credit* are agreements between a bank and a business specifying the amount of unsecured short-term borrowing the bank will make available to the firm over a given period of time
  - A line of credit is not a guaranteed loan, only preapproved credit
  - The bank will usually require cash budgets and pro forma financial statements before approving a line of credit
  - The line of credit usually represents the maximum amount the business can owe the bank at any point in time

16-28 *Lines of Credit and revolving Credit Agreements*

- Lines of Credit have a number of important features
  - Interest rate tied to prime rate
  - Operating change restrictions
  - Compensating balances of 10% and 20%
- *Revolving credit agreements* are lines of credit that are guaranteed to the borrowers by their banks for a stated period of time regardless of the scarcity of money
  - Often made for a period of greater than 1 year
  - A *Commitment Fee* is normally charged by the lender

16-29

Commercial Paper

- **Commercial Paper is a form of short-term financing consisting of unsecured promissory notes issued by firms with high credit standings**
  - **The Maturity ranges from 3 to 270 days**
  - **The Denomination is typically $100,000 or more**
  - **Interest on Commercial Paper is determined by the size of the discount (from par value) and the length of time to maturity**
  - **Annual effective rate = [$ Amount Of Discount ÷ ($ Par - $ Discount)] x (360 ÷ Maturity)**

16-30

Example

- **The Stanley Corporation issued $100,000 of commercial paper that has a 45 day maturity and sells for $99,250.**

    The annual effective rate =

- **The yield on commercial paper is usually 1 to 3 percent below prime. It is a cheap source of funds for firms, yet yields a better-than-normal return for suppliers of short-term funds whose other options are somewhat limited**

16-31   *Commercial Paper*

Commercial Paper is sometimes directly placed with investors by the issuer, or can be sold through a commercial paper dealer who is paid a fee

International Loans

16-32

- **International Transactions**
  - **Often involve the use of a foreign currency and, thus,**
  - **Expose U.S.-based companies to exchange rate risk**
  - **Are often of larger size and longer maturity than domestic transactions**
  - **Generate some reluctance on the part of financial institutions to lend funds, particularly to smaller firms**

Financing International Trade

16-33

- Banks that offer financing for international trade generally use a *Letter of Credit* which guarantees payment of an invoiced amount by the customer of the bank
- Firms that transact business in foreign countries on an ongoing basis often finance at least part of these transactions with funds from banks in the foreign countries, thus minimizing exchange rate risk and enhancing ties to the host community
- Transactions Between Subsidiaries are often accomplished by "netting" amounts due between subsidiaries, thus minimizing foreign exchange fees and other transaction costs

Secured Sources of Short-Term Loans

16-34

- *Secured Short-Term Financing* is obtained by pledging specific assets, usually accounts receivable or inventory as collateral
- A *Security Agreement* specifies the collateral held against the loan, the terms of the loan, interest rate, and other loan provisions
- Although collateral reduces the risk of loss if the borrower defaults, the risk of default remains the same, thus making *secured loans riskier in the view of the lender*

16-35 *Characteristics of Secured Short-Term Loans*

- **Collateral and Terms**
  - Lenders prefer collateral that has a life, or duration, closely matched to the term of the loan
  - Liquid current assets, such as accounts receivable and inventory, are the most preferred collateral
  - The terms of the loan usually include a percentage advance of 30% to 100% of the book value of the collateral, that then constitutes the principal amount of the loan
  - The interest charged is typically higher than on unsecured loans because of the greater risk of default and higher costs of negotiating and administering a secured loan
  - Collateral reduces the risk of loss in case of default, but does not change the risk of default

Institutions Extending Secured Short-Term Loans

16-36

- **Commercial Banks**
- **Commercial Finance Companies**
  - Make only secured loans, both short- and long-term
  - Charge higher rates than do banks because they typically have higher-risk borrowers

The Use of Accounts Receivable as Collateral

16-37

- **A pledge of *Accounts Receivable* involves the use of a firm's accounts receivable as collateral for a short-term loan**
    - **The pledging process:**
        - » **Lender evaluates the accounts receivable to determine their desirability as collateral**
        - » **Lender chooses the acceptable accounts with adjustments**
        - » **Lender typically advances 50-90% of the total dollar value of the acceptable accounts receivable**
        - » **Lender files a *lien* (legal claim) on the collateral**
        - » **As borrower collects the receivables, the loan is paid off**
    - **Pledging can be done on either a *notification or non-notification basis***
    - **Pledging costs are generally high**

Factoring Accounts Receivable

16-38

Factoring Accounts Receivable involves the outright sale of receivables to a factor (bank or other institution) at a discount

Factoring constitutes about one-third of the total financing secured by accounts receivable and inventory in the U.S.

Factoring Agreement

A factoring agreement states the exact conditions, charges, and procedures for the purchase of an account receivable

Factoring is normally done on a *notification basis*, thus the factor receives payment of the account directly from the customer

The factor often makes the credit decision and is responsible for collecting the amount owed, thus assuming all the credit risk (*nonrecourse basis*)

The factor usually pays the firm when the account is collected or on the last day of the credit period, whichever occurs first

The firm maintains an account with the factor in which surplus funds can be left to accrue interest or the factor may make *advances* (loans) funds can be borrowed against uncollected accounts not yet due

16-39   *Factoring Cost*

- Factoring Costs typically include commissions of 1-3% of the book value of factored accounts, and interest rates 2-4% above prime on advances
- Factoring is attractive to many firms because it turns receivables immediately into cash, ensures known patterns of cash flows, and eliminates the need for a credit and collection department

16-40   *The Use of Inventory as Collateral*

■Inventory usually has a market value greater than its book value, but book value is used to establish its value as collateral

■*Marketability* is the most important characteristic of inventory being evaluated as loan collateral

16-41   *The Use of Inventory as Collateral*

- The three key types of inventory loans are:
  - *Floating Interest Lien* which is a claim on inventory in general
  - *Trust Receipt Inventory Loan* which is used to finance relatively expensive inventory items that remain in pessesion of the borrower
  - *Warehouse Receipt Loans* which is an agreement whereby the lender receives control of pledged collateral which is stored or warehoused, by an agent designated by the lender

DISCUSSION PROBLEM

16-42

The J.T. Corporation has a highly seasonal business cycle. Balance sheets for peak and off-peak seasons (in 000's) are on the next slide:

16-43   ## DISCUSSION PROBLEM

	PEAK	OFF-PEAK
Cash	$ 75	$ 15
Marketing Securities	10	20
Inventory	60	15
Accounts Receivable	75	15
Fixed Assets	450	450
	$ 670	$ 515
Spontaneous Liabilities	$ 100	$ 75
Short-Term Debt	120	15
Long-Term Debt	225	200
Common Equity	225	225
	$ 670	$ 515

Is the J.T. Corporation aggressive or conservative in its working capital policy? Why?

16-44   ## DISCUSSION PROBLEMS

■ The Havlicek Company has the following credit terms: 1/5 net 20 EOM. For those customers not taking advantage of the discount, what is the implied rate of interest they are paying?

■ SOLUTION

■ If the Havlicek Company has lax collection policies and no late   penalties on overdue accounts, what is the cost of giving up the discount for a firm paying in 37 days?

16-45   *DISCUSSION PROBLEM*

The Simpson Company is contemplating
two short-term borrowing options.
Bank A will allow them to borrow
$100,000 for one year at a fixed interest
rate of 13.25%, payable at maturity.
Bank B has approved a loan of
$105,000 for one year at a fixed rate of
interest of 11.5%, but interest must be
paid in advance. Which loan should
the Simpson Company take?

16-46   *SOLUTION*

Bank A's interest charge =

Bank B's interest charge =

16-47   *DISCUSSION PROBLEM*

The Harper Corporation, a financially
stable entity, wishes to raise
$1,000,000 to use for the next 90 days.
If Harper sells commercial paper with a
90-day maturity at a 1.75% discount,
what effective annaul interest rate is it
paying for the funds?

16-48   *SOLUTION*

Interest =

[17-1] *Cash and Marketable Securities*

- **Cash And Marketable Security Balances**
- **The Efficient Management Of Cash**
- **Cash Management Techniques**
- **Marketable Securities**

Cash and Marketable Securities Balances

[17-2]

■Cash and Marketable Securities are the most liquid of a firm's assets, creating a pool of funds to be used to pay bills as they come due and to meet unexpected outlays

■ *Cash* is ready currency, either in hand or in a demand deposit account

■ *Marketable Securities* are short-term, interest-earning money-market instruments

■ Temporary "idle" cash is best utilized in the form of marketable securities

17-3 *Motives for Holding Cash and Near-Cash Balances*

Transactions Motive ensures that the firm has enough funds to transact its routine, day-to-day business affairs

Safety Motive protects the firm against being unable to meet unexpected demands for cash

Speculative Motive allows the firm to take advantage of unexpected opportunities that may arise

17-4 *Estimating Cash Balances*

- The *Baumol Model*

$$ECQ = \sqrt{\frac{2 \times \text{Conversion Cost} \times \text{Demand For Cash}}{\text{Opportunity Cost (In Decimal Form)}}}$$

WHERE:

Conversion cost = cost of converting marketable securities to cash ($/conversion)

Opportunity cost = interest earnings given up due to holding funds in a non-interest-earning cash account

17-5

Example

- **The Dotts Company estimates a cash demand of $500,000 for the coming year. It costs $25 to convert marketable securities into cash. The marketable securities earn 7.5% (annualized)**

ECQ =

The total cash demand divided by the ECQ gives the number of conversions necessary during the year to replenish the cash account

17-6

Example

- **The average cash balance is ECQ divided by two**

- **Average Cash Balance =**

17-7

Example

The total cost is the sum of the conversion costs (number of conversions necessary x conversion cost) plus the opportunity costs (average cash balance x opportunity cost)

17-8

Example

- Total cost =

- Cash transfers larger or smaller than the ECQ will result in a higher total cost

17-9   *Estimating Cash Balances*

- The *Miller-Orr Model* estimates cost-efficient cash balances assuming uncertain cash flows by determining an *upper limit* for cash balances and a *return point*, which is the level at which the cash balance is set either when cash is converted to marketable securities or vice-versa
  - Cash balances can fluctuate between the upper limit and zero
  - The parameters for the model are all based upon the return point, calculated as:

$$\text{Return Point} = \sqrt[3]{\frac{3 \times \text{Conversion Cost} \times \text{Variance of Daily Net Cash Flows}}{4 \times \text{Daily Opportunity Cost (In Decimal Form)}}}$$

17-10   *Example*

- Continuing with the Dotts Company, it costs $25/conversion, opportunity cost is 7.5%, and the variance of daily net cash flows is $15,000

$$\text{Return Point} = \sqrt[3]{}$$

The upper limit = three times the return point

=

17-11

Example

- **When the cash balance hits the upper limit, excess cash (in the amount of upper limit - return point) is converted to marketable securities**
- **When the cash balance falls to zero, marketable securities in the amount of the return point are converted to cash**

17-12

Miller-Orr Model

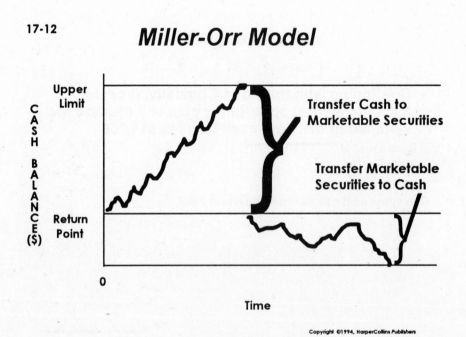

17-13   *The Level of Marketable Securities Investment*

- The marketable securities portfolio serves as a "safety stock" of cash that can be used to satisfy unanticipated demands for funds
- The difference between management's desired level of liquidity and the level of transactional cash balances determined from one of the models is the optimal level of marketable securities investment
- In lieu of a marketable securities portfolio, a firm may use a line of credit to protect against against unanticipated demands for funds

17-14   *The Efficient Management of Cash*

- Cash balances and safety stocks of cash are significantly influenced by the firm's production and sales techniques and by its procedures for collecting sales receipts and paying for purchases

17-15   *The Operating Cycle*

- The *Operating Cycle* (OC) of a firm is the amount of time from the point when the firm begins to build inventory to the point in time when cash is collected from the sale of the resulting finished product

OC = Average Age of Inventory (AAI) + Average Collection Period (ACP)

17-16 *The Cash Conversion Cycle*

- The *Cash Conversion Cycle* (CCC) is the amount of time the firm's cash is tied up between payment for production inputs and receipt of cash from sale of the resulting finished product

CCC = OC - Average Payment Period (APP)

or

CCC = AAI + ACP - APP

Managing the Cash Conversion Cycle

17-17

- A Positive cash conversion cycle means that the firm must use nonspontaneous (i.e., negotiated) financing (unsecured short-term loans or secured sources of financing) to support the cash conversion cycle
- Conversely, a Negative cash conversion cycle is desirable since it allows the firm to use spontaneous financing to support other aspects of the business
- NOTE: Positive cash conversion cycles are far more common

17-18

Cash Management Strategies

- The Three basic cash management strategies are to:

- Turn over inventory as quickly as possible

- Collect accounts receivable as quickly as possible

- Pay accounts payable as late as possible

Efficient Inventory-Production Management

17-19

■Shortening the production cycle and/or increasing raw material and/or finished goods turnover decreases the AAI

■For each day the AAI is reduced, the need for negotiated financing is lowered

17-20 Accelerating the Collection of Accounts Receivable

• Adjusting the credit terms to make it more attractive for customers to pay earlier and/or more expensive to miss paying on time lowers the ACP

• For each day the ACP is reduced, the need for negotiated financing is lowered

Stretching Accounts Payable

17-21

- **Paying bills as late as possible without damaging the firm's credit rating increases the APP**

- **For each day the APP is increased, the need for negotiated financing is lowered**

Combining Cash Management Strategies

17-22

- **Firms generally will implement all three cash management strategies to attempt to reduce their need for negotiated financing**

- **Care must be taken to avoid experiencing excessive inventory stockouts, losing sales due to tough collection policies, and damaging credit relationships due to overstretching accounts payable**

- **Efficient cash management results in a reduced need for negotiated financing and its attendant financing costs**

17-23

Example

- A firm spends $10 million annually on operating cycle investments and pays 10 percent interest for its negotiated financing. If that firm can reduce its cash conversion cycle by 25 days, it will save

- in annual financing costs.

Cash Management Techniques

17-24

- **The firm can minimize its negotiated financing needs by taking advantage of imperfections in the collection and payment systems**

17-25

Float

Float is a term used to describe funds that have been dispatched by a payer but are not yet in a spendable form for the payee, or when a payee has received funds in a spendable form but the funds have not been withdrawn from the payer's account

17-26

Types of Float

- **Collection Float**
- **Disbursement Float**

17-27   *Components of Float*

◆Mail Float
◆Processing Float
◆Clearing Float

17-28   *Float Timeline*

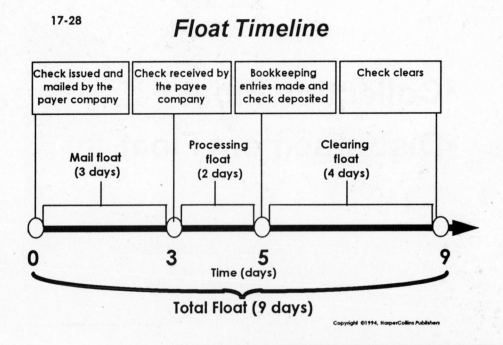

17-29 *Speeding Up Collections*

- **Collection Techniques are designed to *minimize collection float***
  - Concentration Banking
  - Lockbox Systems
  - Direct Sends
  - Other techniques include:
    » Preauthorized checks (PACs)
    » Depository transfer checks (DTCs)
    » Wire transfers
    » Automated clearinghouse (ACH) debits

17-30 *Slowing Down Disbursements*

- **Disbursement Techniques are designed to *maximize disbursement float***
  - Controlled Disbursing
  - Playing the Float
    » Staggered funding
    » Payable-through drafts
  - Overdraft Systems, Zero-Balance Accounts, and Automated Clearinghouse (ACH) Credits

17-31 *The Role Of Strong Banking Relationships*

- For many firms effective cash management begins by establishing a strong relationship with a commercial bank

- Banks tend to look at their commercial customers as profit centers and, thus, have developed many products and services to assist them in efficient cash management

- Banks charge both direct fees and compensating balances for the products and services

- It behooves the financial manager to shop around for bank services and purchase only those that are priced to result in a net gain for the firm

International Cash Management
17-32

- ### Differences in Banking Systems

  - Foreign banks have fewer geographic and service-related restrictions than do U.S. banks

  - Foreign banks tend to use direct payment systems such as *Giro systems* that minimize the need and ability to use checks

  - Foreign banks are allowed to pay interest on corporate demand deposits and routinely provide over draft protection

  - Foreign banks generally charge more and higher fees for their services and often engage in *value dating*, i.e. making deposited funds available for use several days or weeks after they are deposited

International Cash Management

17-33

- **Cash Management Practices**
  - Multinational corporations need to both maintain local currency deposits in each country in which they operate and retain centralized control over all cash flows and balances
  - The use of large international banks to collect and disburse cash and monitor foreign-exchange rates is common
  - Multinational firms can minimize cash requirements and sometimes totally eliminate international payments using *intracompany netting techniques* between subsidiaries
  - Large international cash payments are usually handled by one of the wire transfer services operated by international banking consortia such as the *Clearing House Interbank Payment System (CHIPS)*
  - Multinational firms with excess cash to invest have the flexibility to invest in foreign as well as domestic marketable securities

17-34

Marketable Securities

- **Marketable securities are short-term, interest-earning, money market instruments that can be easily converted to cash**
- **Characteristics of Marketable Securities:**
  - A Ready Market which is defined by:
    - » *Breadth*, or number of market participants
    - » *Depth*, or the market's ability to absorb the purchase or sale of a large dollar amount of a particular security
  - *Safety of Principal*, which means the security is easily sold for close to its initial value

Government Issue Securities

17-35

- **Treasury Bills**
  - $10,000 minimum denomination
  - Sold at a discount
  - Very strong secondary market
  - Low yield
- **Treasury notes**
  - $1,000 or $5,000 minimum denomination
  - Strong secondary market
  - Low yield for length of maturity
- **Federal Agency Issues**
  - $1,000 or higher minimum denomination
  - May have coupon interest or be sold at a discount
  - Strong secondary market
  - Yields somewhat higher than similar maturity Treasury issues

Nongovernment Issues

17-36

- **Negotiable Certificates of Deposit (CDs)**
  - $100,000 is normal denomination
  - Maturities vary, but 30 days is average
  - Yields are based upon size, maturity, and prevailing money market conditions
- **Commercial Paper**
  - $100,000 minimum denomination
  - Maturities vary from 3 to 270 days
  - Yields usually comparable toCDs, but above U.S. Treasury issues
- **Banker's Acceptances**
  - Maturities vary from 30 to 180 days
  - Sold at a discount
  - Low risk because two or more parties may be liable for payment at maturity
  - Yields are slightly below those on CDs and commercial paper, but higher than on U.S. Treasury issues

Nongovernment Issues

17-37

- **Eurodollar Deposits**
  - 75% of these deposits are in U.S. dollars
  - $1,000,000 is the typical denomination
  - Maturities vary from overnight to several years
  - Interest is paid at maturity, but yields are above nearly all other marketable securities
  - Higher risk due to less bank regulation
  - Active secondary market
- **Money Market Mutual Funds**
  - Easy to acquire with low transaction costs
  - $500-$1,000 minimum investment required
  - Liquidity similar to checking account
  - Returns comparable to CDs and commercial paper
- **Repurchase Agreements**
  - Yield is slightly below outright purchase of similar marketable securities
  - Maturities are tailor-made for the firm
  - Provides ideal method to satisfy the transactions motive

DISCUSSION PROBLEMS

- **The Standley Company uses the Baumol Model to determine its transactional cash balances. If the company has an ECQ of $17,500, a $50/transaction conversion cost, makes 40 conversions/year, and can earn 7% on its marketable securities, what is the total cost of this policy?**

SOLUTION

- **Number of annual conversions   =
  x cost per conversion   x**
                                    $

- **Average cash balance = $
  x opportunity cost   x**
                                    $

- **Total cost =**

17-40   ## *DISCUSSION PROBLEM*

- A company using the Miller Orr Model has hired a new assistant financial manager. The financial manager has called in sick on a day that the company's cash balance is approaching zero. The controller tells the new assistant, "Hey you'd better arrange a sale of marketable securities." The only data that the new assistant can find on the Miller-Orr Model is that the upper limit is $36,510. How much should the assistant have transferred?

17-41   ## *SOLUTION*

- ## Return Point =

17-42   *DISCUSSION PROBLEM*

• Given the following financial data for the Smith Corporation, calculate the length of the firm's operating cycle (OC).

Sales	$2,610,000
Cost of Good Sold	$2,088,000
Inventory	$ 278,400
Accounts Receivable	$ 471,250

17-43   *SOLUTION*

• Inventory turnover =

• Average age of inventory =

• Average collection period =

18-1   *Accounts Receivable and Inventory*

- **Credit Selection**
- **Changing Credit Standards**
- **Changing Credit Terms**
- **Collection Policy**
- **Inventory Management**
- **Techniques For Managing Inventory**

18-2   *Credit Selection*

To compete in today's economy most firms extend credit to their current customers and use credit as an incentive to attract new customers

Accounts receivable represent about as 37% of the average manufacturer's current assets and 16% of total assets, making the management of credit an extremely important activity

Accounts receivable are controlled through the firm's *Credit Policy*, which addresses the issues of credit selection, credit standards, and credit terms

Collection policy is another issue that must be addressed by any firm extending credit to customers

Credit Selection is the decision of whether to extend credit to a particular customer and, if so, how much

18-3   *The Five C's Of Credit*

- **Character**
- **Capacity**
- **Capital**
- **Collateral**
- **Conditions**

18-4   *Obtaining Credit Information*

- **Obtaining Credit
  Information is the first step
  in the evaluation process**
  - **–Application Forms**
  - **–Historical Financial Statements**
  - **–External Sources**

18-5 ## *External Sources of Credit Information*

- *Dun & Bradstreet (D&B)* is the largest mercantile cresit-reporting agency in the United States
- Credit Interchange Bureaus can provide firms with factual data regarding the credit history of firms for a fee
- Direct Credit Information Exchanges provide participants with credit information
- Bank Checking may provide vague credit information (from the applicant's bank)

18-6 ## *Key to Ratings*

Key to Ratings

Estimated Financial Strength		Composite Credit Appraisal			
		High	Good	Fair	Limited
		1	2	3	4
5A $50,000,000 to	and over	1	2	3	4
4A $10,000,000 to	49,999,999	1	2	3	4
3A 1,000,000 to	9,999,999	1	2	3	4
2A 750,000 to	999,999	1	2	3	4
1A 500,000 to	749,999	1	2	3	4
BA 300,000 to	499,999	1	2	3	4
BB 200,000 to	299,000	1	2	3	4
CB 125,000 to	199,999	1	2	3	4
CC 75,000 to	124,999	1	2	3	4
DC 50,000 to	74,999	1	2	3	4
DD 35,000 to	49,999	1	2	3	4
EE 20,000 to	34,999	1	2	3	4
FF 10,000 to	19,999	1	2	3	4
GG 5,000 to	9,999	1	2	3	4
HH Up to	4,999	1	2	3	4

DUN & BRADSTREET
Information Services

18-7   *Analyzing Credit Information*

- **Analyzing Credit Information is the next step in the evaluation process**
  - **Procedures**
  - **Economic Considerations**
  - **The Small Business Problem**
- *Credit Scoring* **is a good (and inexpensive) way for   firms extending credit to a large number of small accounts to address credit analysis**

18-8   *Example*

Credit Scoring of Barb Buyer by Haller's Stores

Financial and characteristics	Score (0 to 100) (1)	Predermined weight (2)	Weighted score [(1)x(2)] (3)
Credit references	80	.15	12.00
Home ownership	100	.15	15.00
Income range	70	.25	17.50
Payment history	75	.25	18.75
Years at address	90	.10	9.00
Years on job	80	.10	8.00
		Total: 1.00 Credit score	80.25

Credit Score	Action
Greater than 75	Extend standard credit terms
65 to 75	Extend limited credit; if account is properlyconvert to regular credit after one year
Less than 65	Reject application

18-9 *Managing International Credit*

- ■ The problem of credit management is exacerbated for international companies that must deal with *exchange rate risk* and the dangers and delays involved in international shipping
- ■ When dealing with businesses in developed countries with major currencies an exporter can use strategies (i.e. futures or options) to protect against exchange rate risk
- ■ When dealing with businesses in developing countries an exporter may rely on factors to manage its international export (credit) sales

18-10 *Changing Credit Standards*

- • *Credit Standards* are the minimum requirements for extension of credit to a customer
- • Key Variables
  - – Sales Volume
  - – Investment in Accounts Receivable
  - – Bad Debt Expenses
  - – Summary of Changes and Effects Relaxed Credit Standards

Variable	Direction of Change	Effect on Profits
Sales Volume	Increase	Positive
Investment in A/R	Increase	Negative
Bad Debt Expense	Increase	Negative

18-11   *Determining Values of Key Variables*

- Any change in credit standards will impact all three key variables
- The net marginal change resulting from relaxed, or tightened, standards can be determined by using assumptions regarding the effects of the proposed standards change on sales volume, investment in A/R, and bad debts
  - The additional profit contribution from sales equals the marginal number of units sold times the contribution margin per unit (contribution margin = sale price - variable cost per unit)
  - The cost of the marginal investment in accounts receivable is the difference between the cost of carrying receivables before and after the introduction of a change in credit standards
  - The cost of marginal bad debts is the difference between the level of bad debts before and after the credit standard change
  - Profit contribution, cost of A/R investment, and cost of bad debts rise when standards are relaxed and fall when standards are tightened

18-12   *Making The Credit Standard Decision*

- **The decision to change credit standards should be based on a marginal analysis of the net impact of the change on the three key variables**

Example

18-13

- **Given the following information for the Dodd Tool Company, which is contemplating a relaxation of credit standards:**

Item	Current	Proposed
Sales volume	60,000 units	63,000 units
Ave. Collection period	30 days	45 days
Bad debt expenses	1% (of sales)	2% (of sales)

- Sales price: $10/unit
- Variable cost: $6/unit
- Required return (i.e. opportunity cost on funds): 15%

18-14 *The Effect on Dodd Tool of a Relaxation of Credit Standards*

Additional profit contribution from sales		$12,000
[3,000 units x ($10 -$6)]		
Cost of marginal investment in A/R		
Average investment under proposed plan:		
$\frac{(\$6 \times 63,000)}{8} = \frac{\$378,000}{8}$	$47,250	
Average investment under present plan:		
$\frac{(\$6 \times 60,000)}{12} = \frac{\$360,000}{12}$	30,000	
Marginal investment in A/R	$17,250	
Cost of marginal investment in A/R(.15x $17,250)	($2,588)	
Cost of marginal bad debts		
Bad debts under proposed plan (.02 x$10x 63,000)	$12,600	
Bad debts under present plan (.01 x$10x 60,000)	6,000	
Cost of marginal bad debts	($6,600)	
Net profit from implementation of proposed plan	$ 2,812	

18-15

Changing Credit Terms

- *Credit Terms* specify the repayment terms required of a firm's credit customers
- Cash Discounts
  - Cash Discounts, when *increased or initiated*, generally encourage customers to buy more (volume) and pay more quickly

Variable	Direction of Change	Effect On Profits
• Sales volume	Increase	Positive
• Investment in accounts receivable due to non-discount takers paying earlier	Decrease	Positive
• Investment in accounts receivable due to new customers	Increase	Negative
• Bad debt expenses	Decrease	Positive
• Profit per unit	Decrease	Negative

  - When cash discounts are *decreased or eliminated*, the opposite effects will occur

18-16

Example

- Given the following information on the Dodd Tool Company:

Item	Current	Proposed
Sales volume (in units)	60,000	63,000
Ave. collection period	30 days	15 days
Bad debt expenses	1%	0.5%

Cash discount = 2%
Sale price = $10/unit; Variable cost $6/unit

- NOTE: If the net profit is positive due to the proposed plan, implement the plan

18-17 *TheEffects on Dodd Tool of Initiating a Cash Discount*

Additional profit contribution from sales		$12,000
[3,000 units x ($10 -$6)]		

Cost of marginal investment in A/R

Average investment under proposed plan:

$$\frac{(\$6 \times 63,000)}{24} = \frac{\$378,000}{24} \qquad \$15,750$$

Average investment under present plan:

$$\frac{(\$6 \times 60,000)}{12} = \frac{\$360,000}{12} \qquad 30,000$$

Marginal investment in A/R	($14,250)	
Cost of marginal investment in A/R(.15x $14,250)		$ 2,138
Cost of marginal bad debts		
Bad debts under proposed plan (.02 x$10x 63,000)	$ 3,150	
Bad debts under present plan (.01 x$10x 60,000)	6,000	
Cost of marginal bad debts		$ 2,850
Cost of cash discount (.02 x .60 x $10 x 63,000)		(7,560)
Net profit from implementation of proposed plan		$ 9,428

18-18 *Cash Discount Period*

- The net effect of changes in the Cash Discount Period is difficult to analyze because there are three separate volume changes associated with the investment in accounts receivable

- The anticipated effects of an *increase* in the discount period on the key variables are as follows:

Variable	Direction of Change	Effect On Profits
Sales volume	Increase	Positive
Investment in accounts receivable due to nondiscount takers paying earlier	Decrease	Positive
Investment in accounts receivable due to discount takers still getting cash discounts but paying later	Increase	Negative
Investment in accounts receivable due to new customers	Increase	Negative
Bad debt expenses	Decrease	Positive
Profit per unit	Decrease	Negative

18-19

Credit Period

- **The Credit Period, when increased, has the same effects as a relaxation of credit standards, i.e.**

Variable	Direction of Change	Effect on Profits
Sales volume	Increase	Positive
Investment in A/R	Increase	Negative
Bad debt expenses	Increase	Negative

- **As before, if the net effect on profits is positive due to the credit period change, implement the change**

18-20

Collection Policy

- *Collection Policy* **is the set of procedures for collecting a firm's accounts receivable when they are due**

- **Introduction**
  - Bad debt expenses are a function of both credit policy and collection policy
    - » In general, increasing collection expenditures reduce bad debt
    - » The *average collection period* ratio (Chapter 4) is often used to evaluate credit and collection policies

18-21 *Collection Policy Relationship*

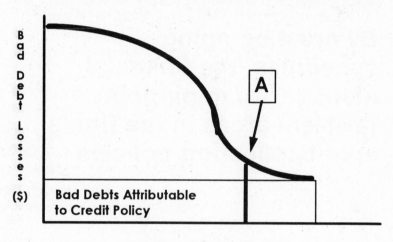

Collection Expenditures ($)

18-22 *Aging Accounts Receivable*

- *Aging* Accounts Receivable is a technique that indicates the proportion of the accounts receivable balance that has been outstanding for a specified period of time
  - A common time increment is 30 days
  - An example of an aging schedule looks like this:

Days	Current	0-30	31-60	61-90	Over 90	
Month	December	November	October	September	August	Total
Accounts Receivable	$60,000	$40,000	$66,000	$26,000	$8,000	$200,000
Percentage of Total	30	20	33	13	4	100

18-23 *Aging Accounts Receivable*

- **By creating aging schedules, the financial manager   can pinpoint problem areas in the firm's credit/collection policies**

18-24   *Basic Tradeoffs*

- There are basic tradeoffs involved with modifying the firm's collection efforts
- For example, an *increase* in collections efforts would likely lead to the following effects:

Variable	Direction of Change	Effect on Profits
Sales volume	None or decrease	None or negative
Investment in A/R	Decrease	Positive
Bad debt expenses	Decrease	Positive
Collection expenditures	Increase	Negative

Types Of Collection Techniques

18-25

- **Letters of Reminder**
- **Phone Calls**
- **Personal Visits**
- **Collection Agencies or Attorneys**
- **Legal Action**

Computerization Of Accounts Receivable Management

18-26

- **Computers are commonly used to:**
  - Bill customers, monitor payments, create exceptions lists, and generate collection letters
  - Assist in credit decisions, such as requests for additional credit by customers
  - Assist the collection department by providing account updates
  - Monitor the effectiveness of the credit department by generating data on the status of outstanding accounts

18-27   *Inventory Management*

- Inventory is necessary to permit the production-sale process to operate with a minimum of disturbance
- Inventory may represent as much as 42 percent of a typical manufacturing firm's current assets and about 18% of its total assets
- Inventory is commonly under the control of the production/operations manager, but the financial manager generally acts as a "watchdog" and advisor in matters concerning inventory

18-28   *Inventory Fundamentals*

- Types of Inventory include:
  - *Raw materials* used in the manufacture of finished products
  - *Work-in-process* which consists of items in production
  - *Finished goods* which are produced but not yet sold
- Differing Viewpoints About Inventory Level
  - Financial Manager: low levels to minimize cost
  - Marketing Manager: high levels to minimize stockouts and maximize customer service
  - Manufacturing Manager: high levels to ensure timely and low-cost production
  - Purchasing Manager: high levels (of raw materials) to secure low cost per unit and ensure ready availability

18-29 *Inventory As An Investment*

- **Inventory requires the firm to tie up money that could be used for other purposes**
- **The larger the average inventory, the larger the dollar investment and required costs such as insurance and handling**
- **Any change in inventory levels must be evaluated from a benefit versus cost standpoint**

18-30   *The Relationship Between Inventory And Accounts Receivable*

- Inventory often becomes an account receivable before it becomes spendable cash
- A decision to extend credit to a customer may increase sales, which will in turn be supported by higher levels of inventory and accounts receivable
- Generally the cost of carrying accounts receivable is less than the cost of carrying inventory since physical handling, storage, and insurance costs are reduced

18-31 *International Inventory Management*

- Complications typically arise in international inventory management due to the logistics of tailoring products for local markets and transporting various forms of inventory long distances and across borders
- The international inventory manager is primarily concerned with having sufficient quantities of materials where and when needed, and in a condition to be used as planned

18-32 *Techniques for Managing Inventory*

- **The ABC System**
  - The ABC System is a technique that divides inventory into three categories of descending importance based on the dollar investment in each category

Group	% of Items	% of Investment	Degree of Control
A	20	70-80	Tight
B	30	10-20	Average
C	50	<10	Loose

  - 'A' group items are controlled on a daily basis; 'B' group items are controlled on a periodic (e.g. weekly) basis; 'C' group items are often controlled by a red-line method under which a reorder is placed when a redline drawn inside an inventory bin is exposed

18-33   *The Basic Economic Order Quantity Model*

- The *Economic Order Quantity* (EOQ) Model is a technique that determines the optimal order quantity of an inventory item, based upon the tradeoff between various operating and financial costs
- Basic Costs include:
    - Order Costs: fixed costs of ordering
    - Carrying Costs: variable costs of holding items in inventory
    - Total Cost: sum of order and carrying costs
- A Graphical Approach

18-34   *A Mathematical Approach*

- Let:

S = Usage in units per period

O = Order cost per order

C = Carrying cost per unit per period

Q = Order quantity in units

- Order cost = O x S/Q
- Carrying cost = C x Q/2
- Total cost = (O x S/Q) + (C x Q/2)

$$EOQ = \sqrt{\frac{2 \times S \times O}{C}}$$

18-35

EOQ

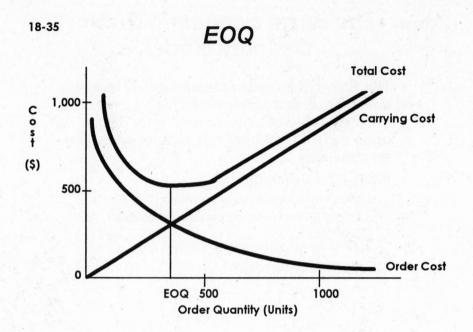

18-36

Example

- **The Luchinski Corporation uses 3,600 insurance forms annually. An order costs $25 to process and carrying costs are estimated at $2 per form per year. What order quantity minimizes total inventory cost? What is the total cost?**

- **SOLUTION**

18-37
The Reorder Point

- The *Reorder Point* is the point at which to reorder inventory, once the EOQ is determined
- Reordering is a function of the daily usage rate of the item of inventory and the "lead time"required to place and receive an order
- Mathematically, the reorder point is expressed as:

  Reorder point = lead time in days x daily usage

18-38
Example

- Luchinski uses 10 forms per day and it takes five days to place and receive an order of forms, thus:
- Reorder point = 10 x 5 = 50 units and Luchinski should reorder when his stock of forms reaches 50
- *Safety Stocks* are extra inventories that can be drawn down when actual lead times and/or usage rates are greater than expected

Materials Requirement Planning (MRP) System

18-39

- *Materials Requirement Planning (MRP)* System is a method of lowering the firm's investment in inventory without impairing production
  - EOQ is used to determine how much to order
  - A computer is used to compare production needs (the "bill of materials") with available inventory balances
  - Orders are generated based upon the time it takes for a product to move through the process of becoming a finished good, and the lead time required to get materials
  - Every dollar released from inventory can be invested to increase the firm's before-tax profits

18-40

Just-In-Time (JIT) System

- A *Just-In-Time (JIT) System* is a method of minimizing a firm's inventory investment by having materials arrive at precisely the time they are needed for use in production
- Ideally, the firm has only work-in-process inventory
- The system is risky since there are no safety stocks and the materials that are used must be of adequate quality
- Obviously, the JIT system requires a considerable amount of cooperation from the firm's suppliers, shipping companies, and employees

18-41   *DISCUSSION PROBLEMS*

- **Through its credit scoring procedures the Klimes Company classifies applicants for credit into groups according to risk. One group that has historically been denied credit has the following group characteristics.**

  » **Average collection period of 59 days**

  » **Bad debt expenses of 7.5% of sales**
  Klimes Co.'s variable costs equal 75% of their products sale price, and the firm requires an 18% pre-tax return on its investment in receivables.
  If this risk group would generate an additional $500,000 in annual sales, should Klimes extend credit?

18-42   *SOLUTION*

A. Additional profit contribution =

B. Cost of marginal investment in A/R =

C. Cost of marginal bad debts =

D. Net profit =

18-43   *DISCUSSION PROBLEM*

The Ruggera Corporation currently has credit terms of "net 30", but is contemplating changing to a policy of "1/5 net 30". The firm anticipates the following effects of this change to be:

- – $100,000 in sales increases
- – Reduction in ACP from 54 days to 42 days
- – 50% of credit customers will take the discount

Ruggera has a contribution margin of 12% (of sales) and annual sales are now $9,900,000. The firm requires a 15% return on its receivables investment. No change in bad debt expenses is anticipated. Should the policy change be made?

18-44   *SOLUTION*

- Additional profit contribution from sales =

- Cost of marginal investment in A/R =
    Present   **Proposed**

- Cost of the cash discount =

- Net profit from policy change =

———

19-1 *Mergers, LBOs, Divestitures, and Failure*

- **Merger Fundamentals**
- **LBOs And Divestitures**
- **Analyzing And Negotiating Mergers**
- **Business Failure Fundamentals**
- **Reorganization And Liquidation In Bankruptcy**

19-2 *Merger Fundamentals*

- **Base Terminology**
  - Corporate Restructuring
  - Merger
  - Consolidation
  - Holding Company
  - Subsidiaries
  - Acquiring Company
  - Target Company
  - Friendly Merger
  - Hostile Merger
  - Strategic Merger
  - Financial Merger

19-3

Motives For Merging

- **The overriding motive is the maximization of owners' wealth, as reflected in the acquiring company's share price**
- **Other specific motives include:**
  - Growth or Diversification
  - Synergy
  - Fund Raising
  - Increased Managerial Skill or Technology
  - Tax Considerations

19-4

Example

- **The Bergen Company has a total of tax loss carryforwards of $450,000. The Hudson Company, which is in the 40% tax bracket and anticipates $300,000 of pre-tax annual earnings, acquires Bergen. Assuming the earnings fall within the annual legal limit allowed for application of the tax loss carryforward, and that the Bergen portion of the merger just breaks even, the taxes and after-tax earnings for the Hudson Company are as follows:**

19-5

Total Taxes and After-Tax Earnings for Hudson Company Without and With Merger

Total taxes and after -tax earnings without merger

	Year 1	2	3	Total for 3 Years
(1) Earnings before taxes	$300,000	300,000	300,000	$900,000
(2) Taxes [.40 x (1)]	120,000	120,000	120,000	$360,000
(3) Earnings after taxes [(1)-(2)]	$180,000	180,000	180,000	$540,000

Total taxes and after- tax earnings with merger

	Year 1	2	3	Total for 3 Years
(4) Earnings before losses	$300,000	$300,000	$300,000	$900,000
(5) Tax loss carry forward	300,000	150,000	0	$450,000
(6) Earnings before taxes [(4) -(5)]	$ 0	$150,000	$300,000	$450,000
(7) Taxes [.40 x (6)]	0	60,000	120,000	$180,000
(8) Earnings after taxes [(4)-(7)]	$300,000	$240,000	$180,000	$720,000

19-6

Mergers

- ## Motives for Merging
  - **–Increased Ownership Liquidity**
  - **–Defense Against Takeover**
- ## Types of Mergers
  - **–Horizontal Merger**
  - **–Vertical Merger**
  - **–Congeneric Merger**
  - **–Conglomerate Merger**

19-7
Purpose of Mergers

MERGER TYPE   PURPOSE

Horizontal   Expand operations in a given product line and eliminate a competitor

Vertical   Gain control over raw materials and/or the distribution of finished goods

Congeneric   Synergy of using same sales and distribution channels for both lines of business

Conglomerate   Reduce risk through diversification

LBOs

19-8

- **Leveraged Buyouts (LBOs)**
  - A clear example of a financial merger, *junk bonds* are practically synonymous with LBOs
  - A typical LBO is financed at least 90% with debt
    » The firm's assets are used to secure the borrowing
    » The lender's take a portion of the firm's equity
  - To be a viable candidate for a LBO, a firm should have:
    » A good position in its industry with a solid record of profitability
    » Low level of debt, but high level of assets to use as collateral
    » Stable and predictable cash flows that are adequate for meeting debt obligations and working capital needs

Divestitures

19-9

- A *Divestiture* is the selling of a portion of a firm's assets for some strategic reason
- Most corporations have operating units, such as a plant, division, subsidiary, or product line, that contribute to the overall operations of the firm
- At times a firm may sell off an operating unit for cash or other productive assets
- Reasons for divestiture include:
  - Generate cash for expansion
  - Get rid of a poorly performing operation
  - Streamline the firm
  - Restructure the firm to be consistent with its strategic goals

Divestitures

19-10

- Divestitures can be accomplished by:
  - Selling a product line to another firm
  - Selling an operating unit to its existing management, often through use of a LBO
  - *Spinning Off* an operating unit into an independent company with its own shares of stock outstanding
  - Liquidating an operating unit's individual assets

19-11   *Analyzing and Negotiating Mergers*

- **Valuing The Target Company**
  - Acquisitions of Assets
    » **Acquisition of Assets is the case in which a firm is acquired for its collection of fixed assets (needed by the acquiring company)**
      - **This is a capital budgeting problem in which the net present value of the acquisition must be computed**
      - **Consider an example, where the Clark Company is considering the acquisition of the Noble Company, a firm with tax loss carryforwards.**

The Noble balance sheet is as follows:

19-12   *Noble Company Balance Sheet*

Assets		Liabilities and stockholder's equity	
Cash	$2,000	Total liabilities	$ 80,000
Marketable securities	0	Stockholder's equity	120,000
Accounts receivable	8,000	Total liabilities and	
Inventories	10,000	Stockholder's equity	$200,000
Machine A	10,000		
Machine B	30,000		
Machine C	25,000		
Land and buildings	115,000		
Total assets	$200,000		

19-13
Net Present Value of Noble Company's Assets

Year(s)	Cash inflow (1)	Present Value factor at 11% (2)	Present Value [(1)x(2)] (3)
1-5	$14,000	3.696	$51,744
6	12,000	.535	6,420
7	12,000	.482	5,784
8	12,000	.434	5,208
9	12,000	.391	4,692
10	12,000	.352	4,224
	Present value of cash inflows		$78,072
	Less: Cash outlay required		75,000
	Net present value		$ 3,072

19-14
Example

p Clark Company needs only machines B and C and the land and buildings.

p Clark Company has estimated cash inflows (after-tax) of $14,000 for years 1-5 and $12,000 for years 6-10 attributable to the assets it will acquire from Noble and the applicable tax losses.

p Additionally, Clark projects an after-tax cash outlay of $75,000.

p If the Clark Company's cost of capital is 11%, should the acquisition be made?

Net Present Value of
The Circle Company Acquisition

19-15

Year(s)	Cash inflow (1)	Present Value factor at 10% (2)	Present Value [(1)x(2)] (3)
1-10	$ 5,000	6.145	$30,725
11-18	13,000	(8.201-6.145)	26,728
19-30	4,000	(9.427-8.201)	4,904
		Present value of cash inflows	$62,357
		Less: Cash purchase price	60,000
		Net present value	$ 2,357

19-16

Acquisitions of Going Concerns

- **Acquisition's of Going Concerns is the case in which a firm is acquired for its income-earning potential**
  - To determine the feasibility of these acquisitions, pro forma income statements reflecting anticipated post-merger revenues and costs attributable to the target firm are prepared
  - If there is a significant difference in the risk behaviors of the two firms involved, the cost of capital resulting from the merger should be estimated and used to discount the relative cash inflows

19-17   *Stock Swap Transactions*

- *Stock Swap Transactions* involve retiring the common stock of the target firm through an exchange of common stock of the acquiring firm
  - The *Ratio of Exchange* is the ratio of the amount paid per share of the target company to the per-share market price of the acquiring firm

19-18   *Example*

- The Huge Company is interested in acquiring the Tiny Company. The acquisition will be consummated with a stock swap transaction. Current market price per share of the Huge Company and the Tiny Company are $50 and $25, respectively. If the Huge Company must offer the Tiny Company $40 per share, what is the ratio of exchange?

[19-19] *Effect on Earnings Per Share*

- **The Initial Effect is typically as follows:**
  - The EPS of the merged firm will be greater than the premerger EPS of one firm and less than the premerger EPS of the other.
  - Analyzing the price/earnings (P/E) ratio paid for the target company's earnings and P/E ratio of the acquiring company gives the following:

[19-20] *Effect on Earnings Per Share*

	Effect on EPS	
Relationship between P/E paid and P/E of acquiring company	Acquiring Company	Target Company
P/E paid > P/E of acquiring company	Decrease	Increase
P/E paid = P/E of acquiring company	Constant	Constant
P/E paid < P/E of acquiring company	Increase	Decrease

[19-21] *Effects on Earnings Per Share*

- **The Long-Run Effect on EPS is a function of the growth of earnings of the merged firm**
  - **The expectation is that earnings will grow in the long-run**
  - **Frequently, however, the earnings attributable to the target firm's assets will grow at a faster rate than those resulting from the acquiring firm's premerger assets**

[19-22] *Effect on Market Price Per Share*

- **Adjustments in the post-merger share price of the acquiring company's stock occur in response to:**
  - Changes in expected earnings
  - The dilution of ownership
  - Changes in risk
  - Other operating and financial changes

- **A *Ratio of Exchange in Market Price* can be calculated using the ratio of exchange:**

$$MPR = \frac{MP_{Acquiring} \times RE}{MP_{Target}}$$

WHERE:

MPR = market price ratio of exchange

$MP_{Acquiring}$ = market price per share of the acquiring firm

MP_{Target} = market price per share of the target firm

RE = ratio of exchange

Example

19-23

- Given the previous example's data for the Huge and Tiny Companies, where Huge sold for $50/share, Tiny sold for $25/share, and the ratio of exchange was .80, the MPR is calculated as:

MPR =

- MPRs are typically more than 1, indicating that the acquisition of a firm generally requires a premium to be paid by the acquirer

The Merger Negotiation Process

19-24

- The Merger Negotiation Process is normally handled by *investment bankers* hired by the acquiring company
- Management Negotiations are initiated when the acquiring firm makes an offer to the target company either in cash or based upon a stock swap with a specified ratio of exchange

NOTE: Nonfinancial issues, such as the disposition and compensation of existing target company management, are negotiated along with the price

19-25

Tender Offers

- **If negotiations with the target company's management break down, the acquiring firm may use a *tender offer* to negotiate a "hostile merger" with the target firm's stockholders**
- **NOTE: A tender offer often takes the form of a *two-tier offer* which makes the terms more attractive to those who tender shares early**

19-26

Fighting Hostile Takeovers

- **Takeover Defenses for fighting hostile takeovers include:**
  - **White Knight**
  - **Poison Pill**
  - **Greenmail**
  - **Leveraged Recapitalization**
  - **Golden Parachutes**
  - **Shark Repellents**
- **Takeover defenses often cause conflicts between a firm's management and its stockholders that result in lawsuits being filed against management**
- **Federal and state governments sometimes intervene to protect the interests of not only stockholders, but also of employees, customers, suppliers, creditors, and others**

19-27   *Holding Companies*

- *Holding Companies* may only need to own a small percentage of the outstanding shares of a given firm to have voting control, since many firms have widely dispersed ownership
  - Advantages of a holding company include:
    - » Leverage Effect
    - » Risk Protection
    - » Some states offer Tax Benefits
    - » Legal actions against one subsidiary do not threaten the other companies
    - » Generally easy to gain control of a firm, because stockholder and management approval is not generally necessary

19-28   *Holding Companies*

- **Disadvantages of a holding company include:**
  - Increased Risk
  - Double Taxation
  - Difficult to Analyze
  - High Cost of Administration

A holding company is sometimes the first step toward a future merger; i.e., if the firms are compatible, a formal combination may later occur

19-29
International Mergers

- Hostile takeovers are virtually non existent
- The emphasis on shareholder value is much lower
- The reliance on public capital markets for financing is much lower
- Only Great Britain's environment is similar to the U.S.'s

19-30
Changes in Western Europe

- Western Europe is moving toward an U.S.-style corporate control and financing model
- The integration of the European economy has fostered many mergers as nationally focused companies attempt to achieve economies of scale in manufacturing and distribution

19-31   *Foreign takeovers of U.S. Companies*

- **European and Japanese companies have been active as acquirers of U.S. firms**
  - It gives them access to the U.S. market, which is the largest, richest, and least regulated in the world
  - It allows them to acquire world-class technology at bargain prices
- **German companies have become especially active acquirers of U.S. companies as the cost of producing export goods in Germany has become prohibitively expensive**

Business Failure Fundamentals

19-32

• *Types Of Business Failure*

- *Technical Insolvency* is a situation in which a firm is unable to pay its liabilities as they come due **(liquidity crisis)**
- *Bankruptcy* occurs when the firm's liabilities exceeds the fair market value of its assets

19-33 ## *Major Causes Of Business Failure*

- **Mismanagement is most common**
  - overexpansion
  - poor financial decisions
  - ineffective sales force
  - high production costs
  - failure to meet competition
- **Economic Activity, such as recessions**
- **Corporate Maturity, as a firm goes through its normal life cycle and eventually declines**

19-34 ## *Voluntary Settlements*

- *Voluntary Settlements* **are arrangements between a failed firm and its creditors that allow it to bypass some of the costs involved in legal bankruptcy proceedings**

- **Voluntary Settlement to Sustain the Firm**
  - The normal rationale for sustaining a firm is to give it an opportunity to recover, if recovery is feasible
  - Strategies for sustaining firms include:
    - » **Extension**
    - » **Composition**
    - » **Creditor Control**
    - » **Some combination of the three preceding strategies**

Voluntary Settlement Resulting in Liquidation

19-35

- Voluntary settlements may result in the firm being liquidated
  - A Voluntary Liquidation usually enables creditors to obtain *quicker* and *higher* settlements than in the case of legal bankruptcy proceedings, but all creditors must agree to the private liquidation
  - A common procedure is to make an *assignment* of the power to liquidate the firm to a third party *assignee* or *trustee*
  - Once creditors are paid off, if any funds are leftover, they are distributed to the firm's owners

Reorganization and Liquidation in Bankruptcy

19-36

Bankruptcy Legislation

- *Bankruptcy Reform Act of 1978* is the current governing bankruptcy legislation in the U.S., made up of nine "Chapters"
  - *Chapter 7* is the portion of bankruptcy law that details the procedures to follow when liquidating a failed firm
  - *Chapter 11* is the portion of bankruptcy law that outlines the procedures for reorganizing a failed (or failing) firm
- When a firm is placed in the hands of the court, the situation is "frozen" so that no one creditor can obtain an unfair share of any settlement

Reorganization In Bankruptcy

19-37

- *Voluntary Reorganization* is a petition for reorganization filed by a failed (or failing) firm on its own behalf
    - This option is not available to municipal or financial institutions
    - Filing a voluntary petition gives the firm temporary legal protection from its creditors
- *Involuntary Reorganization* is a petition for reorganization filed by an outside party, usually a creditor seeking payment of past-due debts
- Any one of three conditions allows an involuntary petition to be filed against a firm:
    - The firm has more than $5,000 of past-due debts
    - Three or more creditors can show aggregate unpaid claims of $5,000 against the firm
    - The firm is insolvent

Steps in the Reorganization of process

19-38

- Filing under Chapter 11 in a federal bankruptcy court
- Appointment of a trustee if creditors object to the firm being a *debtor in possession (DIP)*
- Submitting a Reorganization Plan that is deemed fair, equitable, and feasible by the court
- Acceptance of the Reorganization Plan by the firm's creditors and shareholders
    - Requires approval by creditors representing at least 2/3 of the dollar amount of claims and a numerical majority of creditors
    - Requires approval by 2/3 of the shares of both preferred and common
- Payment of Expenses to those parties involved in the creation and approval (or disapproval) of the reorganization plan

19-39 *The Role of the Debtor in Possession(DIP)*

- Valuation of the firm as both a going concern and as being liquidated to determine which is higher
- Drawing up a plan of reorganization, if the firm's value is greater as a going concern
- Structuring a *recapitalization* to replace the firm's debt with equity or extend the maturity of the firm's existing debt
- Submitting the reorganization plan and disclosure statement to the court

Liquidation in Bankruptcy

19-40

- Liquidation in Bankruptcy occurs if the courts determine that reorganization is not feasible
- Procedures require a court-appointed trustee to liquidate the firm, keep records, examine creditors' claims, disburse money, furnish information as required, and make final reports on the liquidation
  - A meeting of the creditors must be held between 20 and 40 days after firm is abjudged bankrupt
  - A final meeting for closing the bankruptcy is also required

19-41 *Liquidation in Bankruptcy*

- **A Priority of Claims is set by law (Chapter 7)**
  - Expenses of administrating bankruptcy and paying interim bills
  - Wages owed workers (up to $2,000 each)
  - Unpaid employee benefit plan contributions
  - Special claims of farmers or fishermen
  - Unsecured customer deposits (up to $900 each)
  - Taxes owed to federal, state, and/or local governments
  - Secured Creditors receive the proceeds from the sale of those assets pledged to them as collateral
  - Unsecured, or General, Creditors who have a claim against all the firm's assets except those pledged as collateral
  - Preferred stockholders receive an amount up to the par or stated value of their preferred stock
  - Common stockholders are the last in line to receive funds, should there by any left after satisfying creditor and preferred stockholder claims

19-42

Example

- **The Cambridge Company's balance sheet appears at the top of page 795 of your book:**
  The trustee was able to obtain $4.3 million for Cambridge's assets. Given a cost of $800,000 to administer the bankruptcy and pay interim bills, the distribution of funds to creditors holding prior claims is illustrated at the bottom of page 795 of your book.
  The unsecured creditors will divide the remaining funds on a pro-rata basis, (i.e. $700,000/$2,800,000 = 25%; see page 796 of your book)

19-43   **Final Accounting**

- A Final Accounting is completed by the trustee and presented to the bankruptcy court and the firm's creditors
- Once the court approves the final accounting, the liquidation is complete

19-44   *DISCUSSION PROBLEMS*

The Lowry Company is considering acquiring the Dover Company with a stock swap transaction. Currently, Lowry stock is selling for $40/share and Dover stock is selling for $28/share. Lowry's management decides to offer a 1-for-1 swap transaction (i.e. 1 share of Lowry for 1 share of Dover) to the shareholders of Dover Company stock.

What is the ratio of exchange?
ANSWER:

What is the ratio of exchange in market price?
ANSWER:

19-45

DISCUSSION PROBLEM

The Rita Corporation is considering acquiring the Salerno Company for a cash price of $100,000. The management of Rita has estimated the following financial data:

- **Postmerger cash inflows will increase by $15,000/year for five years and by $11,000/year for the following ten years**
- **Postmerger cost of capital will be 13%**
- **Assuming all cash flows are after-tax, should Rita acquire Salerno?**

19-46

SOLUTION

19-47   *DISCUSSION PROBLEM*

The Rafferty Company went bankrupt and was liquidated. There were $3,000,000 of unsecured creditor's claims as follows:

– Unpaid balance of second mortgage $ 500,000
– Accounts payable   250,000
– Notes payable - bank   750,000
– Unsecured bonds   1,500,000
    $3,000,000

• After paying secured creditors and other obligations, the trustee had $1,500,000 left over. How will this be divided among the unsecured creditors?

19-48   *ANSWER:*

20-1   *International Managerial Finance*

- **The Multinational Company And Its Environment**
- **Financial Statements**
- **Risk**
- **Long-Term Investments and Financing Decision**
- **Short-Term Financial Decisions**
- **Mergers And Joint Ventures**

20-2   *The Multinational Company And Its Environment*

- *Multinational Companies (MNCs) are* **firms that have international assets and operations in foreign markets and draw part of their total revenue and profits from such markets**
  - MNCs are becoming more common as world markets become more interdependent
  - The goal of maximizing shareholder wealth, however, is likely to clash with cultural, political, and institutional constraints imposed by operating in foreign environments

International Factors and Their
20-3 Influence on MNCs' Operations

Factor	Firm A (Domestic)	Firm B (MNC)
Foreign ownership	All assets owned by domestic entities	Portions of equity of foreign investments owned by foreign partners
Multinational capital markets	All debt and equity structures based on the domestic capital market	Existence of different capital markets cause opportunities and challenges
Multinational accounting	All consolidation of financial statements based on one currency	Existence of different currencies and accounting rules
Foreign exchange risks	All operations in one currency	Fluctuations in foreign exchange markets can affect revenues, profits, and value

Emerging Trading Blocs: NAFTA
20-4 And The European Open Market

- **NAFTA** *(North American Free Trade Agreement)* extends the free trade zone that has been in effect between the U.S. and Canada since 1988 to include Mexico

- The EC (European Economic Community), a 12 nation bloc representing 350 million people and an overall gross national income similar to the U.S., dropped tariff barriers at the end of 1992 and created what is commonly called the *European Open Market*

20-5   *Legal Forms Of Business*

- **In many foreign countries there are legal forms of business similar to U.S. corporations**
- **To operate in a particular foreign country may require the formation of a *Joint Venture* between a U.S.-based corporation and either private investors or government-based agencies in the host country**
- **Joint venture laws and restrictions have important implications for operating foreign-based subsidiaries**
  - **Many countries require that the majority ownership (at least 51%) be held by domestic investors**
  - **Often disagreements arise among partners regarding the distribution and allocation of profits**
  - **Some countries place ceilings on the return of capital and remittance of profits to MNCs**

Taxes

20-6

- **The Level of foreign taxes is relatively stable among major industrialized nations; may fluctuate among less-developed nations**
- **Taxable Income in some countries is based on a cash basis, while in other countries it is based on an accrual basis**
- **Tax Rates and Rules vary considerably, both in the host country and in the U.S.**

Financial Markets

20-7

- The *Euromarket* which facilitates the borrowing and lending of currency outside its country of origin, is the primary provider for borrowing and lending currencies outside their country or origin
- The Euromarket grew considerably in the last 30 years
- *Offshore Centers* is the name given certain cities or countries that have achieved prominence as major centers for Euromarket business
- New Financial Instruments have emerged in the international financial markets
- Major Participants include:
  - Currencies
  - Banks And Other Financial Institutions
  - Borrowers

20-8

Financial Statements

- Consolidation of financial statements in the United States is based upon the percentage ownership by the parent of the subsidiary

Percentage of beneficial Ownership by parent in subsidiary	Consolidation for financial reporting purposes
0-19%	Dividends as received
20-49%	Pro rata inclusions of profits and losses
50-100%	Full consolidation

Translation of Individual Accounts

20-9

- **Governed by FASB No. 52 which specifies the current rate method**
- **First, each entity's balance sheet and income statement are measured in terms of their *Functional Currency*, which is the currency of the economic environment in which the entity primarily operates and maintains records**
- **Next, the functional-currency-denominated financial statements are translated into the parent's currency using the *All-Current-Rate Method*, which reports balance sheet items at the closing rate and income statement items at their average rates**

20-10

International Profits

- **Covered under *FASB NO. 52* which requires only certain transactional gains or losses to be reflected in the income statement**
- **Income statement risk is dependent upon exchange rate fluctuations**
- **In general, if a subsidiary has a positive income flow, the income statement risk will be positive**

20-11

Risk

- *Exchange Rate Risk* is the risk due to fluctuating exchange rates between two currencies
Relationships Among Currencies
- Major world currencies generally have a *Floating Relationship*, meaning that the value of any two currencies with respect to each other fluctuates on a daily basis
- Many non-major currencies try to maintain a *Fixed (or Semi-fixed) Relationship* with one of the major currencies or a combination of major currencies
- On any given day, the relationship between any two major currencies contains two sets of figures
  - The *Spot Exchange Rate* is the rate of exchange actually in effect that day
  - The *Forward Exchange Rate* is the rate of exchange at some specified future date, and is used to control exchange rate risk

20-12

Impact of Currency Fluctuations

- **The spot and forward exchange rates fluctuate as the result of international forces of supply and demand, internal and external economic elements, and internal and external political elements**
  - If a currency improves its exchange rate relative to another currency, i.e., it now takes less to purchase the equivalent other currency, the situation is known as Appreciation (floating currencies) or Revaluation (fixed currencies)
  - If the inverse occurs, i.e., it now takes more to purchase the equivalent other currency, the situation is known as Depreciation (floating currencies) or Devaluation (fixed currencies)

20-13   *Impact of Currency Fluctuations*

- **A MNC is vulnerable to two kinds of foreign exchange risk exposure:**
  - **–Accounting Exposure**
  - **–Economic Exposure**

20-14   *Impact of Currency Fluctuations*

- **The management of the MNC has to decide how aggressively it wishes to hedge (i.e., protect against) the company's exchange rate risk exposure**

20-15

Political Risks

- *Political Risks* stem from the potential of the host country taking over a foreign firm's assets and operations or implementing specific rules that result in the discontinuity of operations
  - Macro Political Risk
  - Micro Political Risk
  - Coping with political risks
  - While Third World countries have considerable political instability, they also have very promising markets for the goods and services offered by MNCs

20-16 *Approaches for Coping with Political Risk*

Positive approaches:		Negative approaches:
Prior negotiations	**D I R E C T**	License restriction
Prior agreement for sale		control of external
Joint venture		raw materials
Use of locals	**I N D I R E C T**	Control of transportation to external markets
Equity participation		Control of downstream processing
Local sourcing		Control of external markets

See Table 20.4 on page 823 for a full treatment of this issue.

20-17 Long Term Investment and Financing Decisions

- *Foreign Direct Investment (FDI)* is the transfer of capital, managerial, and technical assets from a MNC's home country to a host country
  - If the MNC provides 100% of the equity, it has a wholly owned foreign subsidiary
  - If the MNC provides less than 100% of equity, it has a joint-venture project with foreign participants

Investment Cash Flows And Decisions
20-18

- Due to the various risks previously discussed, it is difficult to measure a MNC's investment in a foreign project, the cash flows from the projects, and the associated risk
- In order to make long-term investment decisions several factors need to be considered
  - The investment a parent company makes in a foreign subsidiary is likely to be valued at the host country's market value
  - Differences in taxes between the parent and host countries can complicate the matter of taxable income and the resultant cash flows from the subsidiary
  - The risks inherent to foreign subsidiaries will impact the discount rate (or cost of capital) the parent company will need to use for evaluating subsidiary cash flows

20-19
Capital Structure

- **Capital structures of MNCs differ from those of domestic firms due to:**
  - International Capital Markets, to which MNCs have ready access, may provide lower-cost sources of long-term financing
  - International Diversification allows MNCs to achieve a greater level of risk reduction and, thus, varying degrees of debt vs. equity
  - Country Factors, such as legal, tax, political, social, and financial aspects, as well as the overall relationship between public and private sectors, can cause differences in capital structures

20-20
Long-Term Debt

- *International Bonds*, which are bonds sold initially outside the country of the borrower and often distributed in several countries, is the most common form of debt
  - A *Foreign Bond* is one sold primarily in the country of the currency of the issue
    - » The Swiss franc is the major choice of currency for foreign bonds
  - A *Eurobond* is one sold primarily in countries other than the country of the currency in which the issue is denominated
    - » The U.S. dollar is the major choice of currency for Eurobonds, but the Japanese yen is growing in popularity

20-21 *Long-Term Debt*

- **The Role of International Financial Institutions**
  - Foreign bonds are normally underwritten by institutions in the countries in which the bonds are issued
  - Eurobonds may be underwritten by any number of institutions in the U.S., Western Europe and Japan, or by an international syndicate of underwriters
    - » Costs are comparable to flotation costs of bonds in the U.S.
    - » Many MNCs create their own financial subsidiaries to raise funds through international bond issues

20-22 *Long-Term Debt*

- **Changing structure of debt**
  - MNCs can alter the structure/characteristics of their long-term assets and liabilities through the use of interest rate and/or currency swaps
  - A common swap involves exchanging fixed-rate payments for floating-rate payments for a given period of time

20-23

Equity Capital

- Equity Issues and Markets
- The MNC can raise equity funds through the international sale of the parent company's stock
  - In 1992, for example, nearly $23 billion of foreign stock was sold in the U.S. market
  - The *Euro-Equity Market* is the London-based capital market dealing in international equity issues around the world
  - An international stock market, potentially capable of competing with New York and Tokyo, is a possibility; however, from the MNC perspective, uniform international rules and regulations for all major national stock exchanges would be necessary

20-24

Equity Capital

- ## Joint Ventures
  - Establishing foreign subsidiaries in the form of joint ventures means that a certain portion of the parent company's total international equity stock is held by foreign owners
  - The political risk in, and treatment of MNCs by, the host country impacts the decision of how much equity versus debt the MNC may wish to have
    - » More Debt from the Host Country makes sense in terms of reducing political risk for the MNC
    - » More Debt from the MNC makes sense if the host country's tax policies (among others) are less restrictive toward intra-MNC interest payments than intra-MNC dividend remittances

20-25   *Short-Term Financing*

- **The usual domestic sources of short-term financing are also available to the MNC**
- **There are several additional foreign sources of short-term financing**
  - The MNC subsidiary's local economic market is a source of funds, both short- and long-term
    » Most local markets and currencies are regulated by local authorities
- **The *Eurocurrency Market* is the portion of the Euromarket that provides short-term foreign-currency financing to MNC subsidiaries**

20-26   *Short-Term Financing*

- **Several currencies can be involved simultaneously**
- **Both *nominal and effective interest rates* - (nominal rates plus (or minus) any forecasted appreciation (or depreciation) - are often involved in investment and borrowing decisions**
- **The MNC will have to consider taxes, intersubsidiary investing and borrowing, periods longer and shorter than a year, the impact on market value, and its response to foreign exchange exposures when making financing decisions**

20-27

Cash Management

* To protect against accounting exposure a MNC can use various *Hedging Strategies*, i.e. techniques to offset or protect against risk

20-28

Exchange Rate Risk Hedging Tools

* **Borrowing or lending**
* **Forward contract**
* **Futures contract**
* **Options**
* **Interest rate swap**
* **Currency swap**
* **Hybrids**

20-29 ## *Cash Management*

- **To protect against economic exposure, a MNC can make Adjustments in Operations**
- **One set of such adjustments would be the manipulation of the subsidiary's operating relationships with other third party firms (i.e. its customers)**
- **Other adjustments involve managing intra-MNC accounts receivable and accounts payable to correct for undesirable foreign exchange exposures**

20-30 ## *Credit And Inventory Management*

- **The global market requires the same credit terms to attract customers as does the domestic market**
- **MNCs must rely upon their home government's assistance in identifying creditworthy customers in the international market**
- **Inventories are subject to exchange rate fluctuations. tariffs, nontariff barriers, integration schemes, and other rules and regulations. In addition, they are sometimes subjected to wars, expropriations, blockages, and other forms of government intervention**

Mergers and Joint Ventures

20-31

- **The same motives that exist domestically for mergers are applicable to MNCs**
  - Growth
  - Diversification
  - Synergy
  - Fund raising
  - Increased managerial skill
  - Enhanced technology
  - Tax considerations
  - Increased ownership liquidity
  - Defense against takeover
- **An important additional motive for international mergers is to allow a MNC to get a foothold in a particular country's market**

Trends

20-32

- Mergers and joint ventures involving European firms acquiring assets in the U.S. increased significantly since the 1980's
- The past two decades have seen tremendous growth in MNCs in the newly-industrialized counties such as Brazil, Argentina, Mexico, Hong Kong, Singapore, South Korea, Taiwan, India, and Pakistan
- Foreign direct investments in the U.S. have been recently popular for investors from Britain, Canada, France, Japan, the Netherlands, Japan, Switzerland, and Germany
- Joint ventures between companies based in Japan and firms from other industrialized nations have been on the rise
- Developing countries have been attracting foreign investment in both horizontal and vertical industries
- International holding companies have been formed in countries with favorable legal, corporate, and tax environments such as Liechtenstein and Panama

NOTES

NOTES

NOTES

NOTES

NOTES

NOTES

NOTES

NOTES

NOTES

NOTES

NOTES

NOTES